Other books by Nick 1

Country

HELLFIRE

The Jerry Lee Lewis Story

by
Nick Tosches

A DELL TRADE PAPERBACK

A DELL TRADE PAPERBACK BOOK
Published by
Dell Publishing Co., Inc.
1 Dag Hammarskjold Plaza
New York, New York 10017

Dell ® TM 681510, Dell Publishing Co., Inc.
Printed in the United States of America
First Dell Trade Paperback printing—February 1982

This work is available in a hardcover edition through
Delacorte Press, 1 Dag Hammarskjold Plaza, New York, New York.

Library of Congress Cataloging in Publication Data

Tosches, Nick.
Hellfire: the Jerry Lee Lewis story.
1. Lewis, Jerry Lee.   2. Rock musicians—
United States—Biography.   I. Title.
ML420.L534T7   784.5'4'00924   [B]   81-12460
ISBN: 0-440-03546-5   AACR2
ISBN: 0-440-53549-2 (pbk.)

For
Michael R. McGovern
a side bet

There is laid in the very nature of carnal men, a foundation for the torments of hell. There are those corrupt principles, in reigning power in them, and in full possession of them, that are seeds of hell fire.

—Jonathan Edwards,
Sinners in the Hands of an Angry God

I'm draggin' the audience to hell with me.

—Jerry Lee Lewis

Acknowledgments

I would first like to thank those people, characters in the tale, who gave of their time and memories: Stella Calhoun, Jack Clement, Carrie Lewis Gilley, Mickey Gilley, Roy Hall, Miss Nellie Jackson, Jerry Kennedy, Eddie Kilroy, B. J. Kirkpatrick, the late Elmo Lewis, Jerry Lee Lewis (*more suo*), Johnny Littlejohn, Kenneth Lovelace, Robert Loyd, Carl McVoy, Rita Mounger, Judd Phillips, Tarp Tarrant, Frankie Jean Lewis Terrell, James Van Eaton, and Marcus Van Story.

I would like to thank Roberta Brandstrader, with whom I skulked through the bottomlands of Louisiana and Mississippi; Al Cooley, alias the Armadillo Kid, for the fanciest footwork in Nashville; Walter Dawson of the *Commercial Appeal* in Memphis; Benny Hickson of Monroe, who gave me much Louisiana history not to be found in any library; Mike Kerr of Mercury Records in Chicago, who, like Jerry Kennedy and Trish Williams of the Nashville office, supplied me with valuable discographical information; the Lloyd sisters, Gwen and Mary, who made my stay in Natchez a memorable one; Joe Nick Patoski, who cased out for me the Southwestern Assemblies of God College in Waxahachie, Texas; and my brother, Richard Tosches, who helped type the final draft of the manuscript when he could have been watching professional wrestling instead.

I would like to thank the staffs of the Concordia Parish Library in Ferriday, the Country Music Foundation Library in Nashville, the Judge George W. Armstrong Library in Natchez, the New York Public Library, the Ouachita Parish Library in Monroe, the Richland Parish Library in Rayville, and the Shelby County Public Library in Memphis.

Most of all, I would like to thank my agent, conspirator, and friend, Russell Galen of the Scott Meredith Literary Agency, and my editor, Morgan Entrekin.

PHOTO CREDITS: page 68, United Press International; 100, Wide World Photos; 106, *London Daily Express;* 126, Wide World Photos; 136, UPI; 154, *London Daily Express;* 157, *London Daily Express;* 159, *London Daily Express;* 160, UPI; 167, UPI; 169, Wide World Photos; 170, UPI; 179, J. R. Brandstrader; 180, Wide World Photos; 192, Mercury-Phonogram Records; 219, Malcom Temple; 239, Art Fein; 250, Charlyn Zlotnick Photography.

It was three o'clock in the morning, and the master bedroom of Graceland was still. Elvis Presley lay in his blue cotton pajamas, dreaming. A small bubble of saliva burst softly at the corner of his lips, and, breathing heavily, he turned. It was the same old dream.

He walked through Tupelo in the late afternoon on a summer's day toward the home of the virgin Evangeline. He was smiling as he turned a corner and entered a street where lush hackberry trees swallowed the sun. There was the house of her father, where she waited, wrapped in that magic, unholy thing from her mama's bottom drawer.

He felt a chill. He was naked. Pleasance became dread, and he flushed with panic. He would retreat across town, where his mother was not dead, and there fetch his clothes. If he hurried, there was time. He took a shortcut through a backyard that he recognized, but he was soon lost, running scared in a strange, unfriendly place until he came to a meadow like none he had ever seen, and afternoon became night and the meadow became endless and he screamed.

The telephone at his bedside was ringing. It was one of the boys downstairs, calling to tell the boss that there was trouble.

Robert Loyd, a Graceland security guard, had watched nervously as the 1976 Lincoln Continental sped up the gravel driveway and struck the gate.

"I want to see Elvis," the driver had shouted, with a voice as harsh as the clangor of chrome and wrought iron that preceded it. "You just tell him the Killer's here."

The guard recognized him and told him that Elvis did not want to be disturbed. This displeased the Killer. He pulled out a .38 derringer, and his eyes, which were already partly closed, tightened with a further wrath.

"Git on that damn house phone and call him! Who the hell does that sonofabitch think he is? Doesn't wanna be disturbed! He ain't no damn better'n anybody else."

Elvis motherfucking Presley—his heart hastened—setting up there in that goddamn mansion pretending he's God, and all he is is some fat old dope addict who dyes his hair like a goddamn woman. As the words of Job admonished: "They spend their days in wealth, and in a moment go down to the grave." To the grave, to the grave, to the grave. He almost laughed, but instead spat in disgust, then commenced howling anew. He did not relent, and the guard went to the phone.

"Elvis says to call the cops," the boy at the house told him. The Killer howled and waved his pistol toward the manor.

The guard did as he was told, and a patrol car arrived in less than a minute. Officer B. J. Kirkpatrick peered into the Lincoln and saw that the Killer had the derringer pressed against the door panel with his left knee. He pulled the door open, and the gun fell. He picked it up and found that it was loaded.

"I'll have your fuckin' job, boy," the Killer hissed.

Kirkpatrick drew him from the car, spread him, frisked him, and locked his wrists. More patrol cars came, and the Killer was taken away.

Riding slowly, against his will, the prisoner glared into the slow river of dark night, wondering what had gone wrong. The thought must have come to him, and just as quickly fled, that there were no Breathalyzers in Old Testament days. This must mean something. He must have thought about singing a song, the old one about meeting in the morning; but he didn't. Then at last he grinned and shook his head, for he knew that the cold, brilliant handcuffs would not long contain him.

A GATHERING OF SHADES

The God of the Protestants delivered them under full sail to the shore of the debtors' colony, fierce Welshmen seeking new life in a new land. From Savannah they traveled westward into the wilderness, across the Canoochee and the Ohoopee, the Oconee and the Flint and the furious Chattahooche, to the Choctaw-cleared thickets of the Alabama Territory. Some stayed there, and some moved west again, farther this time, clear to the Mississippi in a covered wagon, then to the other side, to Louisiana.

"Hell," Jerry Lee Lewis would tell you in the middle of the night, which he seemed to have the power to evoke, to drape about himself, at any hour; "Hell," he would tell you, looking asquint at the veins in his wrist, receding into the memory of his father's tales and the tales of his father's brothers; "Hell," he would tell you, "they got a big history, the Lewises. Wild drinkers. Wild gamblers." Then the final wild son would look away from his veins and regard the whiskey in the one hand, the cigar in the other. "Fuck-ups, I guess," he would say, then laugh or cast an evil murmur, depending on which night he was in the middle of, which cloak he wore.

In Louisiana, on the eastern bank of the Ouachita River, where the city of Monroe now stands, not too far from where the final wild son was born, Jean Filhiol ordered there to be built a fort, in the autumn of 1790, that the settlers of Ouachita Post might be safe from the Chitimachas.

The settlement comprised some two hundred men and women, only seventy-five of whom bore arms. Commandant Filhiol, who had founded the Post in 1785, described his fellow pioneers as "the scum of all sorts of nations." He complained of their indolence and reported that "They excell in all the vices" and that "The women are as vicious as the men." He wrote with embarrassment that "The savages, though savages, who have occasion to see them, hold them in contempt."

The fort was completed in February, 1791, and named in honor of Don Estevan de Miró, the provincial governor who had ordered the establishment of Ouachita Post. By 1800, when the French flag replaced the Spanish in Louisiana, Fort Miro had begun to grow into a town.

It was here, to Fort Miro, that Thomas C. Lewis came about the time that America purchased Louisiana from Napoleon, in 1803. Trafficking in land and law, he became one of the wealthiest and most powerful men in Ouachita Parish. In 1812, when Louisiana entered the Union, Thomas C. Lewis was the parish judge. He and his wife, Lucinda, and their four sons and two daughters lived in a mansion on a bluff overlooking the river. They owned slaves great in number and various in hue, and drank from crystal.

On the first day of May, 1819, the steamboat *James Monroe* came up the Ouachita to Fort Miro. It was the first such boat to visit Fort Miro, and the citizens renamed their town in its honor. Judge Lewis disliked President Monroe, whose name his town had indirectly come to bear, so he decided to secede. He and a neighbor, Patrick Harmonson, obtained through the Fourth Legislature at its first session an act that created from their adjoining properties the town of Lewiston. Though the actuality of Lewiston was ignored and finally forgotten, the town has never been abrogated. To this day, some five hundred acres of Monroe, running north from DeSiard Street along the river, still legally comprise the town-within-a-town that Judge Lewis named in honor of his blood.

In the autumn of 1819, not long after the making of Lewiston, Judge Thomas C. Lewis passed away. His wife followed him in the spring, and the Lewis estate, valued at $8,973, was divided equally among the children.

John Savory Lewis, the great-grandfather of the final wild son, wed a girl named Jane, and, like his father before him, ruled one of the greatest plantations in Monroe. But it was not meant to last. Louisiana seceded in 1861 and fought the War of Independence. The drunkard Grant took Vicksburg, just seventy miles east of Monroe, in the summer of 1863, and John Lewis knew that what his father had wrought from dirt and courage had been wrought to fall, and that his true patrimony was neither the niggers nor the fancy crystal nor the fawning compliance of the townsmen, but only, and supremely, the dirt and courage, which all the ordnance of the North could never wrest from him. In 1865, it fell, as John Lewis had known it would.

"He'd take his fist, hit a horse, knock that horse to his knees. A hell of a man, Old Man Lewis. Then they turned all the slaves loose." This is what the final wild son said of the great-grandfather whom he never knew. He said it as if he were reading an epitaph, and he said it with pride.

Born to the manor in 1856, John Lewis's son Leroy saw the manor fall before his childhood was done. During the years of Reconstruction, many of Judge Lewis's descendants moved to Ruston, a newly founded town some twenty miles west of Monroe. There the Lewises established a wealthy aristocracy of doctors, lawyers, and congressmen, an aristocracy that exists in Ruston to the present day. But Leroy M. Lewis stayed in Monroe. He worked as a clerk in a drugstore, then, for seven years, as a physician's assistant. After that he became a school-teacher, and it was while teaching that he met and fell in love with his fifteen-year-old first cousin, Arilla Hampton. They were married in 1886.

Leroy continued to teach for four years after his marriage, but he grew restless of the city and began to make frequent trips to the wild countryside of Richland Parish, which lay east of Monroe, beyond the Lafourche swamp. His stays in the country grew longer, and finally he bought a farm there. But he had been raised as a city boy, and he did not know how to work a farm. He short-planted his cotton and almost starved.

Leroy and his family moved from one small farm to another until settling finally, in 1909, at a place called Snake Ridge. Located about ten miles southwest of Mangham, near Big Creek, the community of Snake Ridge had been settled by poor farmers in the 1820s. It got its name during the flood of 1828, when William Tom Hewitt, one of the founding set-tlers, saw the ridge protruding above the muddy Mississippi backwater and observed that it was as crooked as a snake. Although Snake Ridge, like its neighbor Nigger Ridge, has nev-er been acknowledged on any map, the old-timers who live there still call the place by the name that William Tom Hewitt gave it back before their daddies were born.

By the time that Leroy Lewis moved to Snake Ridge, Arilla had borne him four sons and seven daughters. On account of all the moving from farm to farm, the children hadn't got much book learning, but they all came to be better farmers than their father, and they all had a gift for making music. Leroy played the fiddle, and his sons played it, too; and the girls loved to play guitar and sing. There was music every night.

Leroy was a good man, but he was a bad drinker, and whatever he didn't ruin by bad farming, he ruined with whiskey. Music was his pleasure when drunk and his penance when sober, and somehow it kept everything from falling apart. He would take that bottle sometimes and ride that New Orleans & Northwestern from Mangham to Rayville, that Vicksburg, Shreveport & Pacific from Rayville to Monroe. He would drink till his mind and his body gave out, and then he would drink some more, till his purse gave out; then he would drink some more, till finally everything that there was to give gave out. Then he would return to Snake Ridge. Singing about Jesus or women without underwear, Leroy M. Lewis would return. And when he did, none was happier to see him than his favorite boy, Elmo.

Elmo Kidd Lewis, Leroy's seventh child and second son, was born on January 8, 1902, in Mangham. Handsome, with fine black hair, a tough jaw, and a grin that reminded his daddy of Old Man Lewis, Elmo was the tallest man in Snake Ridge before he even had call to put a razor to his face. Of all Leroy's boys, Elmo worked hardest and made the best music. He was kind as only a strong man can truly be, but he drank like a weak man. Leroy warned him about this, as he himself had been warned so many times by the Baptist preacher in Mangham. Elmo would just grin. Then his daddy would start grinning back at him. Then that bottle would come out, and Leroy would tell his son about what had come before him: about how Old Man Lewis could knock a horse to his knees with one blow; about the big house on Ouachita Cliff, right where that new Mulhearn Funeral Home was now; about the hundred and fifty slaves and the morning of their freedom, when those slaves walked three miles down the road, turned around, and were back before dinner; and about the dirt and the courage.

Cancer ate Leroy Lewis's stomach, and he died in 1937. By then his favorite son had two little boys of his own. They sat on their daddy's lap, and he touched his face to theirs and told them about what had come before them. Not the part about the dirt and the courage, but the part that was like a fairy tale.

One of the little boys was to perish. The other, upon whom the Lewis patrimony fell, was to rise further than old Judge Lewis himself, further than any of the men in his daddy's tales, before falling even further. He was the final wild son, and he knew it, just as he knew what those men in the tales felt when it thundered but didn't rain.

DIRT

Elmo Kidd Lewis took for his wife a sixteen-year-old girl from the nearby community of Crowville. Her name was Mary Ethel Herron, and she was born on March 17, 1912, during the great flood of that year. Her mother, Theresa Lee, was the daughter of wealthy people, the Foremans, who never forgave their child for marrying John William Herron, a humble farmer with little purse and less ambition. There was a history of insanity in the Foreman family, and Theresa Lee, like her unforgiving father, eventually went mad. It ran strong in the blood, this curse of the Foremans, and could not be cast out by the seed of other blood. Theresa Lee's children, and their children too, would know it. Some would hear it, an evil cawing thing, at certain darkling hours. Others would feel it descend upon them with talons and not fly away.

Mamie Herron was the prettiest, smartest girl that Elmo Lewis had ever run across. Like Elmo, she loved to sing. She was a deeply religious girl, but not so religious as to scare off Elmo. They were married in early 1929. By then many of their brothers, sisters, and friends had left Richland Parish, where life just seemed to get worse each year. Folks there heard about the prosperity that President Coolidge was bringing to America, but they for damned sure knew that none of it was showing up at Snake Ridge. The flood of 1927, when men rowed boats over what had been the cotton fields of Richland Parish, when Mississippi catfish swam through the streets of Mangham, had been the worst flood that anyone there could remember. William Faulkner, who lived on the other side of the river, wrote a book about that flood, a book called *The Wild Palms,* and a lot of people up North thought that he made the whole thing up. Richland Parish was still getting over that flood two years later.

Elmo's sisters Carrie, Eva, and Irene had wed three brothers by the name of Gilley. Carrie and George Gilley stayed at Snake Ridge, but Eva and Harvey, Irene and Arthur Philmore Gilley moved south, to Concordia Parish, to the town of Ferriday. Mamie's elder sister Stella had also moved there, where she was married to Joseph Lee Calhoun, the most powerful man in the parish. With kin and a rich in-law already there, Ferriday seemed to Elmo and his pregnant young bride as good a place as any; so, in the spring of 1929, they packed what little they had and went south, hunting better things.

Ferriday is about fifty miles from Mangham, and back then those miles could be traveled either by rail, on the New Orleans & Northwestern line, or by automobile, on Highway 15. Until 1903 the site of Ferriday had been only a cotton field, part of the Helena Plantation owned by the Realty Investment Company. The location was chosen by the Texas & Pacific and Memphis–Helena & Louisiana railways as a terminal, and in the fall of 1903 the Investment Company laid out the town and named it in honor of the late Judge J. C. Ferriday, whose family had owned the Helena Plantation from 1827 until its sale to the Investment Company at the turn of this century. Ferriday was incorporated as a village in 1906. Governor Blanchard appointed as Ferriday's first mayor one Thomas H. Johnston, who, it has been rumored, duly spent the first week of his office in the town saloon, where he held forth with glee upon the finer points of his proposed Poontang Tax.

For some years Ferriday was little more than a railroad terminal. But by the time that Elmo and Mamie Lewis arrived, it had grown into a community of some 2,500 souls, most of whom were black. (Concordia Parish had always been predominantly black. In the first years after the Emancipation, there had been almost 10,000 blacks and barely 700 whites in the parish. By 1929 white folks had made a comeback of sorts, but the parish was still more than two-thirds black.) Although its streets were not paved, Ferriday had a bank, a brick schoolhouse, gas and electricity, four churches, and the many-splendored King Hotel, where strangers with smooth hands and starched collars spat and talked with local businessmen of Anaconda Copper, New York Jews, four-row cultivators, and accursed wives. Mayor P. H. Corbett liked to say that no honest man could fail to find work in Ferriday. In addition to the cotton farms, there was a hoop company, a cooperage, a lumberyard, and other industry. Three train lines ran through town: the New Orleans & Northwestern, the Texas & Pacific, and the Memphis–Helena & Louisiana. The woods around Ferriday were still rife with wild game: quail and snipe, ducks and doves, deer and coon, even a few bear. It was just like Zion, Mamie told Elmo, except for the niggers and the armadillos.

They settled west of town, out near Turtle Lake, on a farm owned by Joseph Lee Calhoun. Sometimes it seemed difficult to go anywhere in Concordia Parish without treading on Cal-

houn soil. Like old Judge Lewis, whose fallen, acreless off-
spring he came to know, Lee Calhoun was a man for dirt. He
was an unremarkable-looking man, a countryman of medium
build, with a potbelly, weathered skin, and graying hair; yet
he struck as awesome all who knew him. His people had been
settlers in Arkansas, then had followed the Ouachita River
south into Louisiana, past Monroe, forgotten Lewiston, south
to where the Ouachita flowed into the Black. There, in Concordia Parish, in the town of Eva, between the freshwater of
the Black and the swampwater of the Cocodrie, he was born,
on February 20, 1887. There, in Concordia Parish, young Lee
Calhoun bought him some dirt. He sold it and bought more
dirt. He continued to do this, always being sure to sell his dirt
at a greater price than he had paid for it. With the new, free
money, he bought more dirt. By the time he moved to Ferriday, not long before his thirtieth birthday, he owned dirt not
only in Concordia Parish, but in Catahoula as well. He put
rent-houses on some of his dirt, so that tenant farmers would
pay him for the use of that dirt; he raised cattle on some; and
on some he erected oil wells. His power came to be as immense
as his wealth. He himself never ran for political office, just as
he never farmed the cotton on his own dirt; but foolhardy were
those who did run for office in his neck of Concordia without
first seeking his benison, for mayors and congressmen and such
performed for Lee Calhoun a function not unlike that of his
tenant farmers. They might be allowed to work his dirt, for
the benefit of all, but they must never forget whose dirt it was.
He rarely traveled beyond Louisiana, but men came to do business with him from as many far-off countries as there were par-
ishes in his home state; and he never cheated anybody who was
too dumb to eventually realize that they were being cheated.
Whether he was leasing mineral rights to the Texas oil billion-
aire H. L. Hunt or selling a broken-down mule to an even

more broken-down sharecropper, he treated each man with the respect due him. Rich or poor, black or white, he treated them right, just so long as they did not transgress against his dirt; for that was the way it should be, Mr. Calhoun said. Through his marriage to Stella Herron, he came to be the patriarch and benefactor of two families besides his own. They were queer families, but they tilled well and did not covet his dirt too much.

On November 11, 1929, not long after the first frost, a baby boy was born to Mamie and Elmo Lewis, and they named him Elmo, Jr. Mamie said how lucky she was, that she was the only woman in the parish who had two Elmos. She said it about ten or twelve times.

It was a happy winter. The cotton harvest had been good, and it brought a fair price, close to sixteen cents a pound. With some of the cotton money Elmo bought a secondhand Victrola, the crank-up kind. He would sit by the fire, looking at his fine seventeen-year-old wife and his fine young male issue, and he would listen to Jimmie Rodgers sing about how he was going to shoot poor Thelma just to see her jump and fall. Life was better here, Elmo thought, than it had been at Snake Ridge. The wooden rent-house that he and his family lived in was crude and dank. There was no electricity, no running water, no gas for heat or cooking. But this new home, and the woods and the town, seemed to Elmo a place of promise, not dark more than light, not haunted with unseen-bird sounds and the long, lonesome rale of that other, lingering century.

Warm weather came and Elmo worked hard in the cotton field, as he always had. Lee Calhoun would ride by on his big bay stud and look at him—taller than the rest, bending lower and sweating harder than the rest. "That is one working fool," he would say to the horse, and ride on. Elmo himself could never really figure out what it was with him and work, just as he could never truly figure out what it was with him and whiskey. He would say that if a man was going to work, then he should work, and if a man was going to drink, then he should drink, and that was that. He said this, and people liked to hear him say it, but he didn't really believe it, didn't really feel the truth of it the way he felt the truth of other things. He said it because people liked to hear it and because it seemed like something one of those men in the tales might say, and that was as far as it went. It wasn't even his dirt. He knew that. But he would outwork the others from dawn until dusk, and then he would enter his shack and smile at Mamie and at baby Elmo. Yes, Elmo Lewis always walked through a door with a smile on his face, people would say, and they admired him for it. Sometimes, after dinner, after the coffee and the corn pudding, at that hour when the underbrush began to whisper and the sun began to fall and everything seemed to take on the sighing ember colors of all the sadness that ever was, Elmo would wander down to the edge of Turtle Lake. He liked to stand there and not smile and not think. Occasionally, among the cypress and the willows, there would be white egrets or a lone blue heron loitering peacefully in the shallows, not-smiling back at him. Once, standing there, he found an Indian thing, a narrow blade of chipped red flint. And once, standing there, he began to understand what it was with him and work, but not so much that he could put it into words.

The harvest of 1930 was a mean one, for the Depression had knocked the price of cotton down to barely nine cents a pound, the lowest it had been since the turn of the century. Elmo took on carpentry jobs that winter, so that there would be enough food for him and his wife and his issue. The following year was worse yet; Elmo's cotton brought him but a nickel on the pound. The price in 1932 was a mite better, but still way closer to a nickel than a dime. Lee Calhoun was a good man to know during those years. When the wind came too bitterly cold through the slats, Elmo and Mamie would take the child to Uncle Lee's house nearby, where the wind did not enter. Mamie would sit and talk with her sister Stella. Elmo, Jr., would sit and drool with little Maudine Calhoun. Elmo and Lee would sit and eat chicken, and Lee would always ask Elmo how his daddy was doing, whether he was any better or not, and Elmo would always tell him, well, you know, it's just a matter of time. The winters passed, and the sowing times and the hot summers.

In the spring of 1933, Franklin D. Roosevelt came along with the Agricultural Adjustment Administration, telling cotton farmers that the government would give them money if they plowed up what they had just finished planting. Lee Calhoun told Elmo to pay no mind to that damn-fool New Deal cripple talking at people from out of a damn-fool radio. He told him that Franklin D. Roosevelt had taken us off the gold standard, and that was bad enough, but now the fireside-talking fool had gone too far, trying to take us off the dirt standard. Besides, Lee Calhoun told him, he himself had pulled that same plow-up trick on half of Catahoula Parish not five years past, and that's all it was then and that's all it was now— a trick. Elmo let his cotton grow, and he harvested it, and he got better than a dime on the pound for it. He went out and bought just about every record Jimmie Rodgers ever made, and he got good and drunk, and he sang along with them, except the one about the sidetrack and the mainline and the spider going to get his ashes hauled, because that one made Mamie mad and she said that she simply wouldn't have it; and he said that it was a shame that Jimmie Rodgers was dead now, and that he had died so young—only thirty-five, only three years older than Elmo himself was now. It made Mamie nervous, the whole thing. But she did love her husband's voice, and she loved to hear him sing.

Junior, too, was becoming quite a singer. He was five now, and he walked to church every Sunday right alongside his mother and daddy, or, sometimes, just his mother. It wasn't only motherly love that led Mamie to brag on her boy. Everyone in the congregation said that Junior had the voice of an angel and the face to match. They all joked about how little Elmo Lewis and little Maudine Calhoun would surely be courting soon, and Junior blushed.

Lee Calhoun took on a flock of new in-laws that year. Up at Snake Ridge, when Elmo was just a boy, his older sister Ada had married a man named Willie Harry Swaggart. At about the time that Roosevelt was telling everyone to rip up his cotton, Willie and Ada, along with their teenage son, Willie Leon, moved down to Ferriday. The elder Swaggart and his son made their living in the fields, and they fished and they trapped. The son, Willie Leon, was a hot fiddler, and he gathered some extra coin—some of that fool, plowed-up coin—playing country dances on weekends. At one of these dances he met the youngest of the Herron sisters, sixteen-year-old Minnie Bell, who had also moved down to Ferriday, along with Ma and Pa Herron and her married sister Viola, not long before the Swaggarts. Early the next year, 1934, when he was nineteen and she was seventeen, Willie Leon and Minnie Bell married.

Lee Calhoun, who was already beginning to lose track of all the in-laws who had come to dwell upon his dirt, had to back off and think awhile about this latest piece of work. Willie Harry Swaggart had married Elmo's sister. Now Willie Harry's son, Willie Leon, had married the sister of Elmo's wife, who was Willie Harry's sister-in-law and Willie Leon's aunt.

Hellfire, Lee Calhoun thought, if this didn't make Elmo's nephew and brother-in-law one and the same. Then Lee Calhoun got to thinking that he'd be damned if Willie Harry and Willie Leon had not somehow configurated theirselves into brothers-in-law of one another, or maybe an uncle and a nephew, instead of a father and a son; and that if Willie Leon and Minnie Bell had a child, Minnie Bell might somehow wind up as the child's aunt as well as its mother, and its grandfather Willie Harry would likely pan out to be its cousin, and in the end that poor child would be lucky if it escaped without being rendered its own uncle, bedridden grandmother, and long-lost forgotten son. And he, Lee Calhoun, had somehow inherited this whole queer-living, breathing, cotton-farming, marrying, multiplying mess of Chinee arithmetic. He got on his big bay stud and rode fast through the bright, quiet end-of-winter afternoon until he stopped thinking, and then he went home and just sort of looked crooked awhile.

The summer came and went, and cotton brought the best price it had in five years. Junior was growing into a fine boy. Mamie saw her little sister Minnie Bell so pregnant and so happy. It seemed a time for life, and Elmo and Mamie decided to have another child. On a cold, dark night after Christmas, when the Hecate wind shrilled so wildly that dogs barked at it and the roaring whistle of the inbound Iron Mountain could not be heard, the seed took hold.

In January, 1935, not long before Mamie knew that she had conceived, Elmo got himself into trouble with the law. Lee Calhoun was not a drinking man, but he knew that such men were plentiful. He also knew that a bushel of corn was worth only a handful of pennies, but that same bushel of corn made into liquor was worth a handful of dollars, and that nothing would ever change this, neither any fool Prohibition nor any fool Repeal. Lee Calhoun had made whiskey before Prohibition, he had made whiskey during Prohibition, and he was making whiskey now. He handled his whiskey business as he handled his dirt business. That's where Elmo and all those Chinee-arithmetic divide-and-carrys came in.

It was a mighty still, with a fifty-gallon capacity, hidden (but not so much as half of Concordia could help but notice it) in the brush near Turtle Lake on Calhoun dirt. Elmo and Willie Leon Swaggart and a few more male in-laws worked the still. They mixed the corn mash and the sugar, watched over the crib, tended the firebox, tapped the petcock, topped the big tin condenser, and filled the jars. It was good hundred-proof whiskey, and they all swore by it and they all drank it. Sometimes when they were out at the still drinking during a run-off, Lee Calhoun would ride up and ask if they recalled that time they found a big old cottonmouth floating dead in that vat of fermenting mash.

They were all out there that day in January, waiting for the first strong drops of whiskey to drip out of the pee-hole, when something came through the bushes—and it wasn't Lee Calhoun asking about a dead snake.

The federal treasury agents held the men at gunpoint and handcuffed them. One agent tore into the copper part of the still with an ax. The prisoners were herded into the back of a federal pickup, and the pickup pulled out onto a dirt road, heading toward Highway 84. Minnie Bell Swaggart was walking down that dirt road, and as the truck approached her she recognized her husband, Willie Leon, and the several other relatives poking from it, waving at her. She started shouting, waving back at them. The agent who was driving slowed the pickup to a halt and Minnie Bell, who was at this time seven months gone, waddled agitatedly up to the truck, paused to stare for a second at the federal seal on the door, then just looked up at her husband and began to bay. Elmo told her to tell Mamie that he wouldn't be home for dinner, but Minnie Bell didn't hear him, she just kept baying. One of the agents, who was sitting with a shotgun among the prisoners, asked who this woman was.

"That's my wife," said Willie Leon Swaggart.

The agent looked at her belly awhile, then he turned to Willie Leon and he said, "Well, you get her out of here. And if I see you around here a minute longer, you're going to jail like the rest of these here." The agent unlocked Willie Leon's wrists, and Willie Leon jumped down from the truck and walked on down the road with Minnie Bell, turning once to watch as the truck rode off with five of his brothers-in-law.

Elmo and his kin were tried and convicted. Lee Calhoun had no power over the federal people. Elmo and the rest knew this. They also knew that Uncle Lee would take good care of their wives and children while they were gone and that he would see to it that their cotton was sown if they were not back by planting time. Not long before they took Elmo away, Mamie found out for sure that she was pregnant, and she told Elmo, and he left town with a smile on his face, telling her that he would be back sooner than trouble.

The New Orleans Federal Jail was small, crowded, and dank. It held fewer than three hundred prisoners, and most of them, like Elmo, were there for liquor violations. On five forenoons a week, the commissary clerk gave lessons in how to read and write. Every Sunday afternoon at three there was a Protestant service. About thirty lucky inmates received the opportunity to earn up to seven dollars a month by working in the prison rubber-mat factory, under the condition that 75 percent of their pay be sent home each month to dependents. Most of the prisoners just sat around and spat, or thought

Nick Tosches

about the natural inclination of this or that woman toward infidelity. Unruly prisoners were sent below to the solitary confinement unit, a pitch-black, stinking hole overrun with rats and lizards. Elmo told some of the inmates that his grandfather, Old Man Lewis, once owned a piece of Monroe, but none of them seemed to believe him. He cursed at them and did not tell them any more, because they were fools.

By the time Elmo came home in the spring, Minnie Bell had become a mother and Mamie was starting to show a belly on her. The Swaggart child had been born on March 15, and Minnie Bell and Willie Leon had named him Jimmy Lee. He was a handsome baby, with fine auburn hair and his mother's good looks. There was a new copper still, too, that Uncle Lee and some boys had built near Turtle Lake a few hundred yards down from where the old one had been. It was good to be back home in Ferriday in the springtime.

Uncle Lee himself got into some trouble that spring, but fortunately it wasn't federal trouble. He was caught with a truckload of purebreed steers and arrested for cattle rustling. By the day of the trial, he somehow managed to sell the evidence to a Catahoula man. The disappearance of the cattle flustered the young maverick district attorney, but what flustered him more were the eyewitnesses whom Uncle Lee rounded up from among his multitude of perpetual debtors to testify under oath that it was a truckload of horses, not cattle, that Mr. Calhoun had been hauling. The arresting officer said that, yes, come to think of it, those creatures' assholes did seem to be pretty far from the ground. On his way out of the courtroom, Uncle Lee told the maverick boy not to fuck with him ever again in Concordia Parish.

Late that summer, on the night of September 8, Louisiana burned with the news that Huey Long had been gunned down

26

in the corridor of the capitol building in Baton Rouge. Hailed as a savior and friend of the poor, damned as a dictator, madman, and nigger-lover, the Kingfish, as governor and then senator, had, since 1928, ruled Louisiana with a big gun and a loud, profane mouth. Lately it had been said that Huey had his eye on the Presidency, and that he would get it. But now a young doctor by the name of Carl Weiss, the son-in-law of an anti-Long leader, had released Huey's soul with a cheap pistol, only to be felled himself, in turn, and shot through with thirty holes by Huey's enraged guards. The Kingfish lingered at Our Lady of the Lake Hospital for a day and a half, then passed away on the morning of the tenth, softly saying, "God, don't let me die. I have so much to do."

Little Elmo started school at Ferriday Elementary that week, and by the end of the month he had begun to learn to read and write. At night he sat by the fire with his school slate and his chalk, and he tried to make songs like the ones he sang at church every Sunday.

When he was not taken to church on the last Sunday of that month, Elmo, Jr., knew that it must be a special and mysterious day, and it was. On that day, September 29, 1935, at an hour more dark than light, Mamie Lewis heard the first scream of her newborn child. A dog no one had ever seen had been howling outside the window near her bed. Her sister Stella had thrown stones to chase it away, but it had come back. Now, finally, it went off into the brush toward Turtle Lake, and Stella Calhoun never saw it again.

Mamie and Elmo named their child Jerry Lee. "I gave him the name Jerry, and his pa, Elmo, gave him the name Lee," Mamie explained to a Hollywood reporter many years later, when her son had grown into a man of great infamy. "I named him Jerry after a silent-movie star—I can't remember his last

name now—who I was crazy about before I married Elmo."
Like little Jimmy Lee Swaggart's father, Elmo named his son
Lee in honor of the lord of the land.

Cotton prices fell that year instead of continuing to rise, as
Elmo had thought they might. But the Calhoun still was running again, and that brought in some money, as did the odd
carpentry jobs that Elmo picked up. It was a hard winter, like
so many others, but Elmo carried his family through it, as he
had done through all the others. At the time when the men of
Concordia Parish turned their minds toward tilling and de-
rived whatever hope they could from the brief blindness to the
past that seemed to be God's vernal blessing to them and
theirs; at this time, on the ninth day of March, there was another birth in the family. Elmo's elder sister and brother-in-
law, Irene and Arthur Gilley, had a baby boy whom they
named Mickey.

Jimmy Lee Swaggart, Jerry Lee Lewis, and Mickey Gilley:
these were the three cousins, born within the breadth of four
seasons, whose names the town fathers would someday paint
with pride upon signs that told the world, or whatever dis-
placed and devious-cruising part of the world happened to pass
through this fading place on Highway 84, that they were now
entering and being welcomed to Ferriday and that this was the
town where these three cousins had been born. The signs said
nothing of hellfire or salvation—just that this was the town of
these cousins' birth.

Jerry Lee was the most striking of the three children. He
was blond and hazel-eyed, and everyone, especially Uncle Lee,
marveled at the lucent, inexplicable power of those hazel eyes.
"That child," Uncle Lee declared, "has the eyes of a jack-
hawk." Elmo looked into the eyes of his young and wordless
son for many nights before suddenly coming to know why
those eyes seemed so familiar; before suddenly, and with what

in lesser men might be felt as a chill, seeing that those hazel eyes, like the edge of Turtle Lake in darkling, whispering twilight, contained the colors of all the sadness that ever was.

One afternoon, when spring was breaking full, Stella sat and told Mamie about the strange dog, and they wondered at it, as when they were young girls in Crowville they had wondered at other strange things. It meant nothing, they knew.

THE DEVIL IN CONCORDIA PARISH

One

During that spring of 1936, two Mississippi women, Mother Sumrall and her young daughter Leona, came west across the river to Ferriday. They found a vacant lot on Texas Avenue, and on this lot they placed old chairs and benches.

Mother Sumrall and her rife, unsmiling child were crusaders of the Assemblies of God, a Pentecostal sect that had been founded in Hot Springs, Arkansas, in 1914. Like the older Pentecostal sects, which dated to the turn of the century, the Assemblies of God believed in the old-time religion and had no truck with Darwinism and the other foolishness that had crept into Protestantism. Like the older Pentecostal sects, the Assemblies of God believed in the sinfulness of liquor, tobacco, picture shows, dance halls, gambling, public swimming, and life insurance. Women were prohibited from cutting their hair, painting their faces, and wearing trousers, for their bodies were temples of the Holy Spirit, and the Holy Spirit would not be suffered to abide in a whore.

The redeeming power of the whore-hating Holy Ghost was at the heart of Pentecostal religion. When the faithful received it, their minds were overcome and they spoke in unknown tongues. This was the only baptism, they said, and they knew that they were the true-saved kindred of the Apostles, who on that first great day of Pentecost "were all filled with the Holy Ghost, and began to speak with other tongues, as the Spirit gave them utterance." (The Bible also said that the redeemed "shall take up serpents; and if they drink any deadly thing, it shall not hurt them; they shall lay hands on the sick, and they shall recover." Some Pentecostal sects in the more remote parts of the South took to handling poisonous snakes and sipping salvation cocktails, made of strychnine and water; others prohibited all medicine except the laying on of hands, which could cure all sickness.) The original Pentecostal doctrine held that the gifts of the Holy Ghost filled the faithful in an unpredictable and mysterious way, and that a man might not by his own design come to speak in tongues or fall into the trembling trance. But the Assemblies of God diverged from this doctrine and held that sanctification should be more actively and earnestly pursued.

Many Pentecostal sects, such as the Church of God in Christ, were black, but the Assemblies of God was predominantly white. By the spring of 1936 it had grown into the largest of all Pentecostal sects and there were about 150,000 of these Assemblies of God whitefolk running here and running there, chasing after the Holy Ghost. Soon, in Ferriday, there would be a few more.

The Sumrall women were bent over, moving slowly among the chairs and benches, pulling weeds from the lot, when Lee

Calhoun drove by in his truck one afternoon. It was not his dirt that these two queer women were fooling with, but he was nonetheless curious, and he asked Mother Sumrall who she might be and what she might be doing.

"We're fixing to make a church here," said Mother Sumrall, and she wiped sweat from her forehead with the back of her dirty hand. Then she smiled at him, as if she might be indicating to him that he, too, should be smiling at what she had just told him. Lee Calhoun thought she was squinting at him.

"A church," Lee Calhoun said.

"Yessir," she said, "a church."

"We got four of them," Lee Calhoun said, and he was smiling a little now.

"Yessir. I reckon this will make five," she said.

"And who might be financing this here project?" he asked, suspecting for a moment in that part of his brain from which no good came that these women might be some peculiar new form of in-lawry.

"God," Mother Sumrall answered, not smiling at all. "God sent us here, and we're doing his will. We're making a church in obedience to God's will."

"I see," Lee Calhoun said. Mother Sumrall was pleased that he saw, and she tilted her head in justification.

"What church are you in?" asked Mother Sumrall.

"Oh, I go to them all. Baptist, Methodist, Eye-talian, you name it. Yes, ma'am, I'm a churchgoin' fool, I am."

"Well, then you'll want to come to mine," she said warily.

"Well, what sort is it?"

"Assembly of God," she said.

"I can't sing," Lee Calhoun said.

"Mister, you don't have to sing to be saved." Mother Sumrall turned to where her daughter had stopped pulling weeds and was sitting on one of the benches, toying with a rock or some such thing. Lee Calhoun watched the two of them do nothing for a minute, and then he shifted.

"Watch out for them chiggers, ma'am," he said, then drove off down the road, wondering whose dirt that was anyway.

By the time that summer set in, the Sumrall women were conducting services under a tent. At first there was just Mother Sumrall standing there preaching to her daughter, who sat up front on a bench looking as if she were in need of a rock to toy with. As the weeks passed, the people began to look in on the Sumrall services, and eventually Mother Sumrall had herself a congregation of sorts, whom she exhorted to repent and led in songs about the blood and the cross and the glory-bound train.

Willie Leon Swaggart had never been in a church service before, but the music coming from the Sumrall tent on Texas Avenue brought him in, and he was soon playing his fiddle there every week. In time his wife, Minnie Bell, began to accompany him on rhythm guitar, as little Jimmy Lee sat at her feet or on Leona Sumrall's lap. Before long Willie Leon and Minnie Bell were telling all their kin about Mother Sumrall and the Holy Ghost. At Lee Calhoun's fiftieth birthday party, it seemed that there was as much talk of the Holy Ghost as there was of the fancy white-frosted cake. Uncle Lee got dyspepsia and muttered something about how those who had nothing were always so quick to believe in what they couldn't see.

One Saturday night not long after he had buried his daddy, Elmo Lewis sat and tuned the old guitar that he had brought down from Snake Ridge. On Sunday morning he took the guitar and Mamie and Junior and little Jerry Lee over to the tent on Texas Avenue. Not too many Sundays later, Elmo quit the

Baptists, the church of his ancestors, and the Lewises became an Assembly of God family.

The Holy Ghost did not keep Elmo from making whiskey, nor did it save his ass from being thrown behind bars again. In the spring of 1938, he and a few other in-laws were busted out at the Turtle Lake still and sent down to the federal prison in New Orleans.

Things at the prison were much the same as they had been three years before, Elmo discovered, except that the solitary confinement hole was in the process of being closed down and the pay in the rubber-mat factory had been raised to about nine dollars a month. He was in for a longer haul than he had been in for in 1935, but he was allowed to have his guitar this time. He sat and spat, and he traded songs with some of the other inmates. He didn't think that these songs were as good as the ones he already knew. These men, he told himself late one night, were the same fools that were in here last time; only their ugly faces were different. The man whose cell was to the left of Elmo's told him that when he got out next year he was going to move his family across the state line to Texas, to the Rio Grande Valley, because it was easier to farm grapefruit than it was to farm cotton and because Texas law allowed a man to shoot his wife if she lay beneath another man. A Cajun man showed Elmo a picture he had drawn, a picture of two men.

On the bright, hot Saturday afternoon of August 6, while Elmo was still in prison, Mamie Lewis sat with her sister Stella in the kitchen of the new Calhoun house on Louisiana Avenue. The two women and their children had finished lunch, and Elmo, Jr., and Maudine Calhoun went outside to play.

Junior and Maudine walked along the ditch by the side of the Jonesville Highway. Junior was not quite nine years old, but it was already known throughout the family and the town that he had a remarkable gift for singing and writing. As he walked with his older cousin that afternoon, he was singing a song he had written for the next day's Sunday School meeting at the Assembly of God tent. Maudine was in a more playful mood, and when they came to a trailer-truck that was parked at the side of the road, and she saw that the driver had just then entered the cab and was starting the motor, she climbed up on the back of the trailer and held to a hanging chain.

"Come on, Junior," she said. "We'll ride."

"No, I'm tryin' to get my song right," he said.

A car with Arkansas plates and a drunken driver turned a corner and came speeding up behind the truck just as it was pulling out. To avoid hitting the truck, the drunken driver slammed on his brake and swerved off the road to the right. Maudine turned white and her mouth screamed as she saw the car run Junior down from behind and come to a dusty whirring halt upon his broken body in that ditch by the side of the road where they had been walking, singing and talking, a moment before.

The police brought the killing driver before Mamie Lewis. He was falling-down drunk and did not know what he had done. The police asked Mamie if she wanted to press charges. Mamie looked at the drunkard and slowly shook her head, not yet crying.

"No," she said. "We don't do things that way. God will take care of this man in due time."

Many years later the drunkard wrote Mamie a letter, telling her that he had not been able to sleep in those many years, that he was under psychiatric treatment, and that he had quit drinking. He begged for her forgiveness, for any few words that might bring him rest. Mamie threw the letter away and knew she had a friend in Jesus.

Elmo received word that the son who bore his name was dead. The people at the prison would not allow him to go home to his wife. On the morning of his child's funeral, two prison guards drove him in handcuffs to the little cemetery that Lee Calhoun owned a few miles north of Ferriday, near Clayton. The guards would not unlock his wrists, and they stood by with guns as Elmo's restrained hands threw a flower on the small casket. Mamie asked the guards to let her husband spend the night with her and two-year-old Jerry Lee. Without looking her in the eye, the guards said they couldn't. If not the night, then just this day, Mamie implored. Again they said no. When she asked that Elmo be allowed to sit with her for just one cup of coffee and the guards said no, Mamie and Elmo both knew that it was not so much a matter of what these men could or could not do, but rather what they were or were not. Lee Calhoun, in a friendly enough way, asked the guards their names, and he did not forget those names, and he waited for a long time to run into those names again in Concordia Parish.

Elmo was released from prison that fall, not long after Jerry Lee's third birthday. He saw that Mamie was clinging very closely to her remaining child, and he told her that everything was going to be all right.

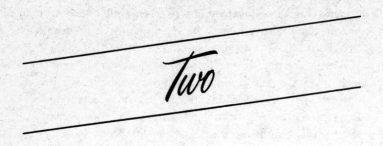

Two

Like the brother he never knew, Jerry Lee was a singing child. To Mamie his voice would never seem as glorious as that of her lost son, but she felt that there was something wondrous, like a fire, in little Jerry Lee's passion for song. She had come from a family that loved music, she was married to a man who loved music, but she had never quite witnessed a love for music as strong and deep as what she saw in Jerry Lee. The child sang in church, and he sang along with his daddy's old records, and he sang along with the children of the black sharecroppers who lived nearby. And sometimes, when he was singing by himself, thinking that no one could hear him, he mixed it all together. Mamie would hear him, and most of the time it made her smile, hearing the child sing those funny, mongrel songs, playing with his voice like that; but at other times it gave her goose bumps, and she would call to him.

One morning she saw him standing with a little colored boy

beneath the window of the shack where the colored boy lived. The two boys were listening intently to the music of a phonograph record that the colored boy's father was playing over and over again. The two boys did not comprehend the song that they heard, but they were mesmerized by the voice that sang it. It was a very painful, very black voice, the likes of which young Jerry Lee had never heard, not even in a dream.

> *There's a hellhound on my trail,*
> *Hellhound on my trail, hellhound on my trail.*

"That man singin', he sold his soul to the devil," the colored boy said. "The devil give 'im that voice."

"Git," said Jerry Lee.

"My daddy told me. You ask 'im. He knew that man who's singin' on that record. They grown up together in Mi'ssippi, in Greenwood, where I's born. That man singin', his name's Spencer, Robert Spencer, an' he sold his soul to the devil, and that's why he sounds like that."

"Git," said Jerry Lee, feeling his heart hasten.

"He's dead now, that man who's singin'."

Jerry Lee said nothing, but began to breathe hard as that voice from beyond the grave seemed to grow louder, blacker, and more painful.

> *Hellhound on my trail, hellhound on my trail.*

"Dead," the colored boy said. "Burnin' in hell."

From where Mamie stood, she heard none of this; but she saw her son turn and run suddenly toward her, into her arms. He wept and told his mother of the dead man who sang with the devil's voice, and she shook her head and prayed to the whore-hating Ghost.

41

Mamie was very dear to Lee Calhoun, and he did not get dyspepsia when she spoke of the Holy Spirit. In 1941 the Assembly of God tent was brought down and in its place was built a fine little white wooden church, paid for by Uncle Lee. Seven panes of glass forming a cross were laid into each of the church's two front doors, and after these doors were planed and hung the Sumrall women moved on to crusade elsewhere. A young preacher named Tom Holcomb was brought in as pastor, but the congregation, which comprised barely thirty souls, most of whom were poor dirt farmers, could not afford to support him. Heeding the advice of the Holy Ghost, Brother Holcomb took a day-job in Texas and commuted on weekends to preach in Ferriday. His young boy died of pneumonia one week, and eventually Brother Holcomb ceased to arrive at the little white church. He was replaced by a quiet, brooding preacher named Henry Culbreth, during the course of whose ministry the Holy Ghost would arrive, for real and with a tongue of cloven flame, in Ferriday.

Jerry Lee started school in the fall after the church was built. It did not take him long to discover that he and book learning were not cut out for each other. His father, however, was adamant about him getting the schooling that he himself had never got. The boy breathed through his teeth and conceived a solution. He would go to school sometimes, which would please his daddy, and the rest of the time he would just pretend that he was going to school, which would please them both. It was a fine system, if he did say so himself.

On those days when he did go to school, he would get together in the schoolyard on Virginia Avenue with his cousin Jimmy Lee Swaggart, who was already in the second grade. Jimmy Lee's home was not a happy one. In the winter of 1939, his family had moved from Ferriday to Rio Hondo, Texas, but not long after they arrived in Texas, Jimmy Lee's baby brother, Donnie, who was barely a month old, died of pneumonia. The family buried the infant and returned to Ferriday. The dead baby tore at its mother and father from beneath distant dirt, and they fought constantly. It was for this reason that Jimmy Lee looked forward to church on Sundays, for at church his parents did not fight. After World War II broke out in December, when Jerry Lee had been in school three months, Jimmy Lee left again for Texas, where his parents found work at a defense plant in Temple. This move did not last long either, and the Swaggarts returned to Ferriday the following year, using the money they had earned to move into a larger house, a house that had everything but electricity, on Tyler Road.

The war years were good for the farmers of Concordia Parish. Cotton prices were higher than they had been in all of Elmo's married years, rising steadily to well over twenty cents on the pound by the end of the war. It was not like the war that Elmo's daddy had told him about, the war that had wrested all but the dirt and the courage and left Old Man Lewis like a wolf in burnt woods. This was a war that a man could get behind, a good twenty-cent-cotton war, where the enemy looked different from you and stayed the hell out of Vicksburg. Lee Calhoun told Elmo that this was nothing, that the harvest following the end of this war mess would bring prices like he had never seen, just as had happened back after World War I, back when Elmo was still a boy. He said that after a war there is always a rush on cotton and women, and then he said something very coarse and both men laughed, but Lee Calhoun laughed louder.

During the war years, traveling evangelists were plentiful throughout the South. These men were the most powerful and fiery of the Pentecostal preachers. They told stories of unspeakable sins and wondrous redemption, of the wrath of God and the mercy of Jesus, of the powers of Satan and the never-end-ingness of hell. They yelled of being saved and of being damned, and of the no-in-between. They took from the purses of the saved and of the damned, and in the name of the Holy Ghost they put into their own; then they praised the Lord and moved on down the line.

Although the Lewises and the Swaggarts and the Gilleys were devout members of the Assembly of God congregation, none of them had yet taken to speaking in tongues, nor did their pastor encourage them to do so. Elmo's sister Ada Swaggart had visited a Pentecostal camp meeting back in Snake Ridge, and she returned to Ferriday speaking in unknown tongues and telling her kin of the experience. Her grandson Jimmy Lee, who spent a great deal of time at her house on Mississippi Avenue, was swept away by her story, and day after day he asked her to tell it to him again. And she would tell him, and, as she told him, the power would fill her and she would begin to speak in tongues, and Jimmy Lee would sit there by her and feel something thrillful creep over his skin. Her other kin thought that the woman had gone crazy, and Jimmy Lee's daddy, Ada's own son, forbade the boy to visit her.

Then one morning in the summer of 1943, the Lewises and the Swaggarts and the Gilleys went to the Assembly of God church to attend a revival being held by a traveling evangelist named J. M. Cason. A few blocks from the church, Jerry Lee and Jimmy Lee and their little friends Mack and Huey P. Stone were playing a game with a stick and a can. Suddenly they heard a loud howling scream cut through the quiet fore-noon. Jimmy Lee recognized the scream as his mother's own, and he flushed. The other boys ran toward the church to inves-tigate, but Jimmy Lee demurred and instead ran home to hide.

When Jerry Lee arrived at the little white church, he saw and heard things he could never forget.

Brother Cason had given an altar call and was leading the congregation in singing. Returning from the altar, Mamie Lewis saw that those around her had begun to jump and shout. She heard her younger sister, Minnie Bell Swaggart, howl and rush from her seat. Mamie Lewis felt herself leap into the air and turn back to the altar. Her sister-in-law Irene Gilley was kneeling before Brother Cason, and she was shouting in an unknown tongue. Mamie fell to the floor of the church and lay there. When she rose she was speaking urgently in a language she had never heard. Minnie Bell danced past her, singing in a different language of her own. Her husband, Willie Leon, was on his feet, grinning and shouting and crying. The unknown tongues became louder, more frenzied, gushing from the church like a sea and frightening away the swallows from the nearby trees. Women rolled in the aisle, overtaken by the Holy Ghost, and men stomped their heels and spun, conversing with God in languages like dry thunder and the breaking open of all things. The traveling evangelist fell to his knees and praised the Lord, and there were tears on his face.

The little white Assembly of God church was never quite the same after the congregation began to speak in tongues. Later that same summer, young Jimmy Lee knelt at the altar and started to speak in a strange language. He spoke very little English for days after that. His mother sent him to the post office for a three-cent stamp. Jimmy Lee placed a nickel on the counter and tried to tell the man what he wanted, but it wouldn't come out in English, only the unknown tongue, and he had to go home without the stamp. Of course, his mama understood and was not angry. Jimmy Lee could not get enough of the Holy Ghost once he started speaking in tongues.

Out behind his house he made a log altar in the midst of a clump of trees, and every day he knelt there and prayed for many hours.

Jerry Lee did not build an altar behind his house. He continued to carry out his great compromise scheme of education. On some mornings he would sneak off by himself, toward the woods or toward the town. He would linger by the tar-shingled juke joints where bad black people drank in the morning, and he would listen to the music that came from the nickel machine. He would hear the voices of men who had sold their souls to the devil, and he would watch the effect that those voices had upon the men who drank and listened.

"What you want, boy, squirrelin' 'round here like you do?" one of the drunken black men asked him one morning.

"I like to listen to the juke, is all," Jerry Lee replied defensively.

"Shit," the black man said. "Ain't but a mess of tore-down niggers howlin' at the moon."

"You ever see the Devil?" whispered Jerry Lee.

"Ever' time I drink, boy, ever' time I drink." The man laughed, then turned and walked away.

At home in the evening, Jerry Lee would try to make the jukebox music on his daddy's guitar, and he would mix it with all the other music he carried around in his head. On other mornings he would board the yellow school bus and put in his time, listening to some old woman who barely recognized him tell him and the other, more familiar faces all about Eli Whitney and how Christopher Columbus walked around with a ball under his arm trying to find somebody to believe him. A girl named Rita who rode the bus to school with Jerry Lee on those occasional mornings of his great compromise complained to her mama in a giddy, flattered way about how he would strut down the aisle of the bus with those holes in the knees of his jeans and stick that face full of freckles right up to her face and say with that sly grin of his, "Is this seat saved?"

The great compromise scheme was not without its problems. At the close of his third-grade year, in the spring of 1944, his teacher, Mrs. West, handed him his report card. He looked at it. There were a lot of *F*'s. He started counting them with his eyes, making a small sound with his tongue as he counted each one, but he stopped when he reached twenty. Then he saw where it said that he had not been passed and must start all over again in the third grade next fall. He walked from the school and stood on Virginia Avenue, feeling as Columbus must have felt after he had been scuffling around all those years with that damned ball under his arm. No, worse than that even.

Jimmy Lee Swaggart, who had just been passed to the fifth grade, saw him standing there like a blind boy whose dog had just run off, and he asked him what the trouble was. Jerry Lee handed him the report card, and Jimmy Lee looked at it. "Let's talk to the teacher," he said. "I know her. She taught me last year." They went back into the schoolhouse, and Mrs. West explained to Jimmy Lee that his cousin had not come to class for any of the tests. Jimmy Lee said that, yes, he knew that, but it was because Jerry Lee's folks were forced to move so frequently. "He studied hard at home and he knows all the material," Jimmy Lee said, then turned to Jerry Lee: "Isn't that true, Jerry?" And Jerry Lee nodded, grateful that his cousin was speaking in English, then looked at the teacher and said, "My father will kill me if I go home with this report card. He'll kill me." Jimmy Lee assured the teacher that this was the truth, that she did not know his cousin's parents, that they surely would kill their son as quickly as they would cut a hog. Mrs. West took the report card and looked at it for a moment, and then she looked at the two boys. She took an ink eraser from the desk drawer and began to rub and whisk away several of the *F*'s, then she took her fountain pen and put *D*'s where the *F*'s had been, and she passed Jerry Lee Lewis to the fourth grade without for one second believing anything that these boys had told her, but feeling herself nevertheless moved by them.

The report card still had too many *F*'s on it as far as Elmo was concerned. He took his son and held him with one great hand, and with the other great hand he unlatched his belt and whipped it free from his britches. He brought the son and the belt together many times so that they made a nasty stropping sound, and he cursed indolence, until finally Mamie yelled to him, "Elmo, stop, you're killing that child," and he stopped and let his son go.

Jerry Lee, Jimmy Lee, and Mickey were close that summer. The cousins often rode bicycles into nearby Vidalia. Sometimes they walked out along the catwalk of the Natchez-Vidalia Bridge, which spanned eight thousand feet across the Mississippi River. Jerry Lee would climb over the railing and perch on a ledge, waving at passing motorists. Sometimes he would crawl out onto one of the girders and, clutching it, lower himself over its edge until he dangled high above the deadly rushing waters. He would hang there, feeling the blood beat hard and fast in his ears and in his chest, feeling the wild thrillsome chill fill his lungs as the light and dark within him made his fingers with their occult warring ache and twitch, and he would hear Mickey and Jimmy Lee holler with fright, yelling for him to come on back.

He had once asked his daddy why the dead of Ferriday were not buried beneath the dirt of Ferriday. Elmo had explained that the dead must be buried in high ground, beyond the reach of the Mississippi floodwaters, for those raging, wicked waters would wrench the coffins of the dead from their graves and send them whirling and shattering and tumbling in the terrible muddy torrents, and that this was something that neither the dead nor the living should be made to suffer. Jerry Lee must have thought of this as he hung there, caressed sinfully, maternally, by the warm breeze of the killing baptismal waters' surging. But most of all he must have thought, or rather wondered, about the fear that drove him to dangle in purgation from those girders, and whether his fear was greater or lesser than his cousins', which held them, or maybe saved them, from even nearing the edge of the catwalk.

"Git on back here, Jerry, git on back here!" his cousins would call.

"Come and git me," he would howl. "Come and git me."

They rode up to Clayton, too. This was not so much a town as it was a cluster of wood and brick houses built around a cotton gin. Jerry Lee's brother, Elmo, was buried in the lush hills outside Clayton in soil owned by Uncle Lee Calhoun. Sometimes Jerry Lee would pedal along the rough dirt road that led to the little cemetery among the trees. He would stand there and look at the small limestone marker and the little stone lamb that surmounted it, and he would read the words that his mother and father had inscribed in memory of the brother he never truly knew:

BUDDED ON EARTH TO BLOOM IN HEAVEN

The silence of this place enwrapped him and the little stone lamb and the lovely words, and lent mystery to that preached-of darkness that lay fast below him in the even greater silence of Lee Calhoun's dirt.

Near the Tensas River, not far from the little cemetery, were several groups of Indian mounds upon which had long ago stood the ceremonial temples of the Taensa tribe. These earthen mounds by the fast-running, lucent river were all that remained of the Taensa, and they comprised an area that was known locally as Indian Village. Jerry Lee and his cousins played often among these mounds where the obscure Taensa worked their magic. Jerry Lee learned to throw a knife here. It was a skill he would never lose. The boys saw deer and rabbits and possum in great numbers here, and in certain twilights they saw what old black men who lived near Clayton called the Chief.

On most days Jerry Lee and his cousins would stay in Ferriday. They would swim in Lake Concordia, which was at the eastern edge of town, across the railroad tracks. When they had money they would go downtown to Vogt's Drugstore and buy ice cream cones and comic books, which were all they ever read. Jerry Lee and Mickey enjoyed the matinees at the Arcade Theatre on Louisiana Avenue. They saw just about every Western picture there was to see, wishing always afterward that the war would end so that Gene Autry, who was their favorite, could get out of the air force and back in the saddle again. Jimmy Lee did not go to the picture shows with his cousins. He had been in line one afternoon waiting to pay his quarter to Mrs. Green, the old woman at the ticket window, when he heard a voice speak to him. "Do not go in this place," the voice said. "I have chosen you as a vessel to be in my service." He began to cry, and he obeyed the voice.

All three cousins loved music, and all three of them took to the piano. There was an old piano in the Assembly of God church, and Brother Culbreth encouraged the boys to use it on those days when the church was empty, telling them that they would someday be able to perform at services. There was also a piano at Lee Calhoun's house. Uncle Lee and Aunt Stella had bought the piano for their daughter, Maudine, but she didn't really care for it. Much to the Calhouns' pleasure, Jerry Lee came to the house and sat at their piano more days than not. He bent over the keys and tried to figure out where to put his boyish fingers so that they would make the sounds that were in his head. Then he tried to get his fingers to move around so that he could make the sounds come together close enough for a piece of song. Uncle Lee and Aunt Stella, Elmo and Mamie, they all encouraged him. "That's good," they would say. "I couldn't do that."

Mamie was pregnant then, in those warm days of 1944, and it was not long till she gave birth, on October 27, to her first daughter, a ravishing, dark-haired girl child named Frankie Jean. And it was not long till Jerry Lee, sitting at Uncle Lee's piano, figured out what he had been wanting to figure out.

Three

The moment he heard it, the very moment he heard himself
make that song like he had been trying to make it—and he
had been trying to make something that was fine; not just
something that would seem fine coming from an eight-year-
old boy with freckles and stuck-out ears, which he knew he
was, but something that would seem fine coming from the
nickel machine in one of those drunk-morning juke joints, or
from his daddy's Victrola, or from a radio; something that
would seem fine coming from any of these, and yet had not,
because it was different—the moment he heard it, he abruptly
spun around, as if a door had just slammed shut behind him in
an empty room, and he looked straight at Uncle Lee Calhoun,
who was sitting there in that big chair of his with his potbelly
sticking out, looking right straight back at him, and they sat
there like that, the two of them, peering at each other from

opposite ends of lifelong stubbornness, and they broke into grinning and laughing, each in his own way.

The first song that Jerry Lee could play straight through the way he wanted was the nineteenth-century Christmas carol "Silent Night," and he played it in a boogie-woogie style. Elmo was so proud of his son that he borrowed money against what worldly possessions he had, and he drove to Monroe, that place of tales, and he purchased a used Starck upright piano, and he hauled it back down to Ferriday in his pickup truck, and he dragged it into his home and set it before Jerry Lee.

This was in early 1945. The Mississippi flooded that year, and it was the worst flood since 1927. Downtown Ferriday was inundated, and many of the townsfolk had to evacuate their homes and take refuge in a tent camp at the Lake Concordia levee. The war ended that year, too, just a few weeks before Jerry Lee's tenth birthday. As Lee Calhoun had predicted, cotton prices rose to more than thirty cents on the pound during the following year.

Now that Jerry Lee had a piano, he attended school even less frequently than he had in the past, and he suffered less at home for his poor grades. Both Elmo and Mamie were confident that their son would be a great music-maker, though from the very beginning Mamie hoped and prayed that Jerry Lee would dedicate his talent to the Holy Spirit.

In the summer of 1945, Mamie's elder sister Fannie Sue and her family came to visit from Pine Bluff, Arkansas. At the age of fifteen, Fannie Sue had married a nineteen-year-old man named John Glasscock, who became a Pentecostal preacher not long after the marriage. They had a fourteen-year-old son named Carl, who had been born in Epps, Louisiana, on January 3, 1931. Like most preachers' sons, Carl played piano, and this interested his younger cousin Jerry Lee a great deal. Carl told Jerry Lee that he performed regularly at his daddy's church, but once in a while he leaned a little bit on the boogie and that made his daddy madder than hell. He sat down at Jerry Lee's Starck upright and began to hit some Holy Ghost boogie, and sure enough his daddy shot him a nasty glance from across the room.

"They'd bought an old piano," Carl recalled many years later, after he had become known by a different name, "and moved it in that old shotgun house. It was the sort of piano you'd have trouble giving away. I came in there and played the fire out of the thing. Jerry couldn't play too well then. When we left, he came back to Pine Bluff, Arkansas, with us for the summer. He stayed with us about a month and a half, and he made me play the piano every day. When he left to go home, he could do everything I could do. He just had that knack. He didn't have those big fingers yet—he couldn't hit those octaves—but he knew the boogie. It was great."

Jerry Lee sat at his Starck upright every day for hours at a time. He practiced what some people called boogie-woogie and others called the Devil's music. Two of his favorites in these early years were "Down the Road a Piece," which had been a hit boogie-woogie record in 1940, and "House of Blue Lights," which Jerry Lee learned from a record of piano player Freddie Slack right after it came out, in 1946. He practiced both these songs continuously, and from them he learned to keep a fast, heavy rhythm going with his left hand while he played melody with his right. The more he practiced, the surer the left hand and the wilder the right hand became. Jerry Lee also practiced Jimmie Rodgers songs and Al Jolson songs, which he learned from his parents' records; but these, in Jerry Lee's mind, were more for singing than for the fingers. From the Jimmie Rodgers records Jerry Lee learned to blue-yodel, and from the Al Jolson records he learned the power of vocal audacity. (His favorite Jolson record was "Down Among the Sheltering Palms.") He played old Tin Pan Alley tunes, too, such as "In a Shanty in Old Shanty Town," which had been one of the most popular songs of the Depression; but he took a whip to these tunes and shook them down to boogie-woogie, as he had done with "Silent Night." And he always learned the latest Gene Autry songs, such as "You're the Only Star (In My Blue Heaven)," which also became a reconstructed boogie-woogie song in the hands of young Jerry Lee.

In the autumn of 1946, Mamie Lewis became pregnant for the last time. On July 18, 1947, she gave birth to another dark-haired daughter, whom she and Elmo named Linda Gail. By this time, Elmo had installed electrical wiring in his house. (For water, however, the Lewises still had to go outside to the well.) He purchased a radio, from which Jerry Lee absorbed music of every sort. He listened to the popular dance bands that were broadcast by WWL in New Orleans. He listened to the Mississippi bluesmen whose records were played by WMIS, right across the river in Natchez. On Saturday nights he heard "The Grand Ole Opry," routed from Nashville by way of WSMB in New Orleans. Whatever he heard, he swallowed it, then he spat it out on that old Starck upright.

On the first Saturday night of April, 1948, KWKH in Shreveport, the most powerful Louisiana radio station north of New Orleans, introduced a country-music program called "The Louisiana Hayride," which was patterned after, and in competition with, "The Grand Ole Opry." Jerry Lee was listening to the "Hayride" one Saturday night the following August when a twenty-four-year-old man from Alabama named Hank Williams made his debut. Hank's voice grabbed Jerry Lee and sent shivers through him, as the Holy Ghost had sent shivers through others he knew. He had already made up his mind that Jimmie Rodgers and Al Jolson were the two greatest singers who ever were. Now he placed this new Hank Williams fellow right up there with them. Hank became the most celebrated singer on "The Louisiana Hayride," and Jerry Lee listened for him every Saturday night, wondering what he looked like and resolving that he must someday meet him. Occasionally Hank Williams would get drunk and out of hand. Horace Logan, the man in charge of the program, would fire him. Jerry Lee would listen to the show for Saturday night upon Saturday night, wondering where Hank had gone to; then, always, Hank Williams would return, saying, "Howdy, neighbors, it's mighty good to be back." Jerry Lee went to the Starck upright and practiced whatever songs he heard Hank sing. The best one of all, he thought, was "Lovesick Blues," which Hank first sang on the "Hayride" sometime after Christmas. It was an old song, copyrighted in the spring of 1922. The lyrics had been written by Irving Mills, a Jewish immigrant from Russia, and the music had been composed by a vaudeville pianist named Cliff Friend. The song had been recorded several times in the twenties, and in 1939 it was cut by an Alabama-born country singer named Rex Griffin, from whose record Hank Williams had learned the song. But Hank let everyone believe that the song was his. To Jerry Lee's thinking, it was a perfect song, a song that both Jimmie Rodgers and Al Jolson might have recorded. Listening to Hank sing it, Jerry Lee knew that he must ask Hank, on that day when they met, where he stood on Jimmie and Al. Eventually Hank's fame grew too large for the "Hayride" to contain him, and in the spring of 1949 he moved north to the "Opry." Jerry Lee followed him with a turn of the dial.

Jerry Lee's cousins Jimmy Lee Swaggart and Mickey Gilley had also been working at the piano. All three boys now performed occasionally at the Assembly of God meetings, as Brother Culbreth had once said they would. Of the three boys,

Jerry Lee was by far the best, but Jimmy Lee showed a prodigious gift as well. Unlike Jerry Lee, however, Jimmy Lee devoted most of his talent to the Lord, who had claimed him as a vessel, and did not spend much time practicing worldly music (although, if you took the words away, there were more than a few Pentecostal hymns that would not sound foreign coming from the nickel machine in the wildest juke joint). But, sometime after his thirteenth birthday, Jimmy Lee began to backslide, and he and Jerry Lee began to make forays into the slow river of dark night.

On Fourth Street, in the black part of Ferriday, there was a wooden nightclub called Haney's Big House. It was owned and operated by a colored man named Big Will Haney. In those days segregation in the Deep South was a two-way street, and whites were no more welcome in black clubs than blacks were in white clubs. At Haney's Big House the only whitefolk allowed were the disc jockeys from WMIS in Natchez, and they were set off and restricted to a table at the side of the stage.

The finest bluesmen in the South came to Haney's Big House. There were old, established piano players, such as Sunnyland Slim and Big Maceo. There were younger men who had just begun to make names for themselves, men like Muddy Waters, who just a few years back had been working in the cotton fields across the river. There were wild new dance bands, such as Roy Milton and His Solid Senders, Memphis Slim and His House Rockers. Then there were some very young men in their teens and twenties whom no one had yet heard of—men such as Ray Charles, Bobby Bland, and Blues Boy King. The late forties were the most exciting years of black music, for it was then that rock 'n' roll was being born. Old rhythms merged with new, and the ancient raw power of the country blues begat a fierce new creature in sharkskin britches, a creature delivered by the men, old and young, who wrought their wicked music, night after dark night, at Haney's Big House and a hundred other places like it in the colored parts of a hundred other Deep South towns. The creature was to grow to great majesty, then be devoured by another, paler, new creature.

It was to Haney's that Jerry Lee and Jimmy Lee, blond and pubescent, did sneak. In the *Concordia Sentinel,* the weekly newspaper published in Ferriday, there was a column called "Among the Colored," which Jerry Lee examined every Friday when the paper came out to see who would be coming to Haney's Big House the following week. He and Jimmy would steal away from their homes and bicycle down to the bad part of Fourth Street.

"We'd go down there," Jerry Lee recalled years later, after the Big House had fallen. "We'd go down there and sell newspapers and shine shoes and everything, and we'd keep on doin' it until nobody was lookin', and then we'd work our way through the door, y'know. And them cats is so drunk they couldn't walk. And, man, we'd sneak in there and old Haney, he'd catch us. He'd say, 'Boy, yo' Uncle Lee come down heah and *kill* me and you both!' And he'd throw us out. But I sure heard a lot of good piano playin' down there. Man, these old black cats come through in them old buses, feet stickin' out the windows, eatin' sardines. But I tell you, they could really play some music—that's a guaranteed fact."

On some nights Jerry Lee and Jimmy Lee snuck out but did not go to Haney's. They broke into stores downtown and robbed them. Whenever they did this, they would stop by the police station the next day and ask Police Chief Harrison if there was any news about the thieves. "Well, boys," he would say, "we ain't got 'em yet, but we're on their trail." They would ask the chief how many men he figured were involved. "It's a gang of 'em," he would say.

The boys began scheming a big heist as they went about their night thieving. Under one full moon they stole some scrap iron from Lee Calhoun's backyard. They later sold it back to him, and this may have been the only time Uncle Lee was taken in a transaction. Another night they busted into a warehouse at the edge of town, expecting to find all manner of worldly spoil. Instead they found more rolls of barbed wire than they had ever imagined to exist—nothing but rolls and rolls of barbed wire. Jimmy Lee took a roll of it, but discarded it on the way home.

Then one night Jerry Lee went off into the dark without his cousin, and he busted into a store and took some jewelry, and he got caught. This cost Elmo and Uncle Lee a few hundred dollars to straighten out, and it convinced Jimmy Lee that the Holy Ghost was giving him one last chance to vessel-up.

Not long after this incident, Elmo moved his family out of Concordia Parish, south to West Feliciana Parish, where he had been offered a good-paying construction job in Angola, at the state penitentiary.

Angola had once been a great cotton plantation. In 1869 it was purchased by Major Samuel Lawrence James, who transformed the plantation into a brutal, profit-making prison, which he personally operated until his death in 1894. At the turn of the century, the state of Louisiana purchased the Angola prison from the Major's heirs, running it in much the same cruel way as the old Major himself had. Prisoners were shackled, underfed, horsewhipped, and forced to slave-farm cotton on the prison's rich bottomland. In 1946 Governor Jimmie H. Davis, who had been elected to office two years before largely on the basis of his song "You Are My Sunshine," instituted a long-range program to modernize and humanize Angola. Part of this plan called for the removal of all women prisoners from the penitentiary. Another part called for the construction of a new receiving station, classification center, and hospital; and this was the part of Governor Davis's program that brought Elmo Lewis and his family to Angola in 1948.

The Lewises moved into wooden quarters outside the walls of the penitentiary. Jerry Lee and his little sister Frankie Jean attended a slat-patched old school along with the children of the other laborers. It was at this school that Frankie Jean learned to read and write. On the few occasions when Jerry Lee showed up for class, he was relieved to hear no mention of Columbus and his loathsome ball.

Now, Jerry Lee at this time had neither use nor liking for any girl-creature too young to wear an undershirt, and he regarded his sisters not so much as kin or even flesh, but rather as dark-haired, wailing thorns. Frankie Jean was the greater of the thorns, for she was larger than baby Linda Gail and she not only wailed but also spoke. One afternoon Jerry Lee had him an idea. It was the finest idea he had devised since the invention of the great compromise.

His mother had been pleading with him all day to take Frankie Jean outside and play with her. Finally he inhaled through his teeth and dragged the thorn from the house, letting the screen door slam weakly behind him. Frankie Jean climbed into her baby sister's stroller and commanded Jerry Lee to take her for a ride. It was then that he had his idea.

He pushed Frankie Jean for a long while, across dirt and grass and stones, toward a hill that dynamite and steam shovels and bulldozers had recently cleft in twain to make way for a new road. He pushed her to the top of this progress-ravaged hill, to the edge of this barren cliff that God never made. He peered into the chasm, to the moved-mountain rubble many feet below. Then he gave the stroller one final push and heard the scream of the thorn.

The stroller teetered, then plummeted from the cliff. It smashed against a jutting rock and burst into a noisy shower of flesh and hardware. Chrome, cheap wood, and pink tatters sprayed outward and downward in myriad wild trajectories. And in the middle of this crashing, splintering tumblement: the spinning, wailing thorn. It was a glorious sight, and Jerry Lee beheld it.

When he returned home alone, his mother asked where Frankie Jean was. He did not reply, so she asked him again.

"A chicken hawk," he answered. He unscrewed the lid from a jar of peanut butter and stuck in the two longest fingers he had. "Biggest one I ever seen. Snatched her up like a poor little chicklin' hen and carried her off." He squinted upward and raised his hand, the one with the peanut butter on it—raised it toward the heavens and moved it in a long, slow arc, like an Indian in a movie. "Stroller and all."

Frankie Jean entered the house, bleeding and bruised and wailing from the abyss. Mamie grabbed a broom handle and took it to her son until he, too, was bruised; but he would not wail. Frankie Jean did not smile again until she was twelve years old, when she was married.

For a long time after this, there was enmity between Jerry Lee and Frankie Jean. One day Jerry Lee brought home a grasshopper with a broken leg. He fashioned a splint from a match stick and tied it to the insect's leg with black thread. Then he set the grasshopper on the floor—and out leaped Frankie Jean, upon it with one small foot, reducing the creature to an unholy stain.

On a certain night Jerry Lee pretended an armistice and offered to tell Frankie Jean a bedtime story. Frankie Jean lay in bed, and Jerry Lee leaned back beside her and folded his hands behind his head. He closed his eyes.

"Once upon a time, there was this little girl and she was comin' after me." Then he was silent. Then he said, "She's comin' after me." Then he was silent. Then he said, "She's comin' after me." He continued this for some time in the darkness. Frankie Jean was frightened and she pleaded with him to stop, to tell the story right. But all he said was, "She's comin' after me." Frankie Jean knew that Jerry Lee had nosebleed problems, so she drove her little fist straight into his nose and made it spurt blood—made it spurt blood all down his shirt, all over the bed, all over the floor of that little wooden house. They came together like pit dogs, and Elmo separated them.

Some girls, older girls, were not thorns. At Angola thirteen-year-old Jerry Lee discovered romance, and their names were Nell and Ruth. He never forgot those first girl friends, as he never forgot that Starck upright.

Elmo had hauled the piano to Angola, and Jerry Lee continued to make his boogie every day. But here Jerry Lee encountered new distractions: Nell and Ruth, of course, and football. The boys at the slat-patched school in Angola formed a team, and Jerry Lee, who was small but fast and a good receiver, became a running-back and the star of the team. The girls idolized him, and he did too. He loved to watch them press their knees together, watch their eyes cloud like hothouse grapes when they talked to him after the games. One afternoon Jerry Lee was running with the ball toward the thirty-yard line. A *big* sonofabitch came at him, and Jerry Lee leaped sideways into the wintry air. When he came down, he busted his hip and tore his thighbone from his pelvis.

The doctor at Angola put him in a cast from the waist down, and Jerry Lee cursed the hog that ball had been made from. For two months he had to be carried to and from the Starck upright. Because of the cast on his right leg, he was forced to play the piano with that leg stuck out at an angle. He became so used to playing like this, with that leg stuck out, that he continued to sit at the piano in this odd way for the rest of his life. Frankie Jean was assigned the chore of placing a pillow beneath Jerry Lee's busted leg after Elmo had deposited him on the piano stool. She sometimes raised his leg higher than she had to, until he screamed with pain. "I'll kill you, girl, I'll kill you," he would say, then wince into his boogie with wrath.

Elmo packed his family and left Angola in the summer of 1949, returning to Ferriday, to a bigger house, on the Black River. By the end of that summer Jerry Lee knew that he could make music as fine and wild as anything he had heard at Haney's Big House. He was ready to turn professional, and he did.

Four

In June of 1949 two Ferriday businessmen, G. D. Babin and Lloyd T. Paul, opened a Ford dealership on Fourth Street. On the Saturday morning of November 19, less than two months after Jerry Lee's fourteenth birthday, Babin-Paul Motors held an open-house celebration to announce the new 1950 Ford models. Outside in the car lot a hillbilly band was playing, and in the audience were Elmo and Jerry Lee. Elmo told Lloyd Paul that his boy here, Jerry Lee, could play that old piano up there better than that hillbilly who was playing it now. Lloyd Paul was a good-natured man, and he told Jerry Lee to go on and sit in. Jerry Lee strode up to the band, and the piano player moved aside with a grin and a nod to Mr. Paul.

Earlier in the year, Jerry Lee's cousin Maudine Calhoun had given him a record called "Drinkin' Wine, Spo-Dee-O-Dee" by a colored singer named Stick McGhee. The record, which featured some tough piano work by Big Chief Ellis, had been a big hit among blacks and had been covered by Lionel Hampton, jump-blues shouter Wynonie Harris (who also had a rhythm-and-blues hit with it), and even an obscure country band called Loy Gordon & His Pleasant Valley Boys. Jerry Lee loved the record, and he had worked up a fast version of it. Now he sat before the crowd in this car lot with his leg stuck out, and he ran his right hand like lightning down the keyboard, as if to announce himself, and he began to pound the piano and sing "Drinkin' Wine, Spo-Dee-O-Dee." That boy, that fourteen-year-old boy, sat there, rocking, howling a song that was about nothing but getting drunk and fucking up, and all the people there started howling along with him, loving it. For that boy, that fourteen-year-old boy up there, was making the sort of music that most folks had only heard in conjunction with the Holy Ghost, but the boy wasn't singing about any Holy Ghost. He was singing something he had taken from the blacks, from the juke-joint blacks, but he had changed what he had taken, not so much the way someone might paint a stolen pickup to hide his theft, but rather the way that Uncle Lee had changed those cattle into horses: changed it by pure, unholy audacity. And he had changed it into something that shook those whitefolk, something that would have shaken Leroy Lewis and Old Man Lewis before him. And he was doing it, that boy not old enough to shave, right out in the open, in broad daylight. And as he was doing it, Lloyd Paul was running among the crowd with a felt hat in his hand, and people were putting coins into the hat. When Jerry Lee quit playing, Lloyd Paul gave him what was in his hat—almost thirteen dollars. Jerry Lee and Elmo lugged that great jangling mass of copper and silver home in a sack and poured it on the table before Mamie, and they grinned and laughed through their noses like highway thieves as they beheld it: hosanna.

It was not long before Jerry Lee quit high school altogether, to stand on his own, in patrimony. But one part of his school days he would never shake loose was the nickname he had acquired: Killer. "That's what all my friends called me," he explained many years later, long after the world had become accustomed to calling him by that nickname. "I hated that damn name ever since I was a kid, but I been stuck with it. I don't think they meant it *killer* like, like I'd *kill* people. I think they meant it music'ly speakin'. But I am one mean sonofabitch." Although he did grow to hate the name, he also clung to it at times, as he clung to the notion of Old Man Lewis knocking that horse to its knees with a single blow, as Old Man Lewis and Leroy Lewis and Elmo Lewis themselves had clung to such things—courage, dirt, work, an unwrestable grin, and like covenants with one's own pride and will. Yes, although he grew to hate the name in later years, he would remain the Killer forever.

He quit school, but he did not quit church. In the months following the Ford lot show, he and Elmo would load the Starck upright onto the bed of the pickup and roam through the parish, stopping here, stopping there. Jerry Lee would make his music and gather a crowd, and Elmo would pass the hat, and at the end of the day they would split the money. Jerry Lee loved to do this—he loved to play—but it tore at him. Making the Devil's music for money went against all that his church had taught him to be right, all that his mother had wished him to be. But still he did it, and still he suffered for it, and the more the music took hold of him, the more it became a part of him, the more he suffered, until it sometimes got to where he felt the good and the bad, the Holy Spirit and the Demon, so crowding his lungs with their battle that it was hard to breathe. But still he did it.

Between the time of the Ford lot show and his fifteenth birthday, Jerry Lee rose to local fame. A man named Lonnie

Lewis, who was no relation to Jerry Lee's family, owned several small supermarkets in nearby Vidalia and Natchez. Lonnie Lewis was so impressed with Jerry Lee's talent that he arranged for Lewis Supermarkets to sponsor a twenty-minute radio spot for Jerry Lee every Saturday at WNAT in Natchez.

In the first week of March, 1950, when Concordia Parish lay beneath the worst flood it had been hit with in five years, Jerry Lee traveled north to Monroe, the town of his ancestors, to compete in a Ted Mack amateur show, a benefit for the Heart Association, at the Neville High School auditorium. He did not win the contest (Ted Mack's shows inclined more toward harmonizing quartets and tap-dancing daughters than toward young men who played dark night music in a tempo suggestive of procreative panting), but he did win a mention in his hometown newspaper. Under the heading "Jerry Lewis on Amateur's Program," the *Concordia Sentinel* of March 10 informed its readers of the recent benefit show in Monroe and of the fact that "Among the contestants was Jerry Lewis, of Ferriday." All those who were not already aware of Jerry Lee were further informed that "Jerry is a popular pianist and in great demand for appearances over radio and shows."

A few weeks later, on April 3, Elmo gave a public performance of his own, and once again a member of the Lewis family won mention in the hometown newspaper, this time beneath the heading "Ferriday Murder Trial Set in May":

> The case of Elmo Lewis, 40 [he had begun to lie about his age], charged with the attempt to murder his brother-in-law, Lee Calhoun, prominent property owner in the Ferriday and Black River section, has been set for the first week in May during the spring jury term in seventh district court at Vidalia.
>
> Lewis allegedly chased his brother-in-law in an auto-

The mother, the son, the father (Memphis, January, 1959).

mobile with a gun in the vicinity of Ferriday following a dispute over alleged non-payment in the transfer of some Ferriday real estate from Lewis to Calhoun.

Because of the prominence of the persons involved, the case is expected to draw a large audience when it comes to trial. Lloyd Love is attorney for the defendant while the state's case will be argued by District Attorney D. W. Gibson.

The *State of Louisiana* v. *Elmo K. Lewis* never went to court. After a postponement in May, Elmo and Uncle Lee reached an understanding concerning the dirt in question, and the charge was dropped.

A few days after the indictment had been filed against Elmo, a record shop opened in downtown Ferriday next to the Recreation Billiard Center. Mrs. B. F. Ramsey, the proprietor of the shop, stocked all the latest rhythm-and-blues records ("We will appreciate your patronage, white or colored," her advertisements stated), and Jerry Lee became a regular customer, buying up records and devouring them till they came back out through his fingers and his mouth, turned wilder and newer by the fight within—till what came out got to be so fine and good and evil that he often felt not like Jerry Lee Lewis, but like the Killer.

On the Friday night of May 12, Elmo drove Jerry Lee and Jimmy Lee to a talent show in nearby Jonesville. Of the thirty-five contestants, most of whom were full-grown men, Jerry Lee won the first-place prize. Jimmy Lee Swaggart also did well, but he was distressed by the experience, and on the way home he pondered the chill that had rippled down his spine as he played worldly music in front of that Jonesville crowd.

"For the first time in my life," he said, "I sensed what it felt like to be anointed by the Devil."

They rode through the blackness, the two cousins, in the back seat of Elmo's car, feeling between them the presence of an intruder. Jimmy Lee brushed his cornsilk hair back with his hand. This was only the second week of May and already the nights were hot. Elmo steered on, regarding his nephew in the rearview mirror.

A few weeks later, on June 7, the Arcade Theatre showed a picture called *Bob and Sally*. The advertisements in the paper stated that the movie would be presented separately to male and female audiences, and that nurses would be in attendance for the faint of heart. Also:

IN PERSON: THE RENOWNED EXPONENT ON SEX
HYGIENE!
ROGER T. MILES
THE MAN WHO CALLS A SPADE A SPADE!

This was an event that very few young men in Ferriday dared to miss. Jimmy Lee Swaggart was one of the few, for he knew that Roger T. Miles was no friend of his. The boy ran that summer—from God, from Satan—and he continued to run for three years more, until finally he ran, falling, into the arms of some blinding-bright thing, and he never left those arms—never.

Like his cousin, Jerry Lee also knew fear and anxiety. (Only Mickey Gilley, it seemed, was not wracked by temptation and guilt. He knelt together with his mother and spoke in tongues and did not lie with the night as his cousins did.) The more Jerry Lee became involved in music, the more unrest befell him. It was not only the sinful music itself, but also the sins that the music seemed to beget. There were nightclubs, thievery, and girls who unbuttoned themselves. Perhaps the Assembly of God preacher could see these things, as one with true eyes could see rain in a dry sky.

With the help of his mother and his minister, Jerry Lee made an attempt to straighten up and fly right. He decided to give his life to God, to wash the stains from his flesh and start anew.

Five

Southwestern Bible Institute had since 1943 occupied some seventy acres on the northern edge of Waxahachie, the seat of Ellis County, Texas, a rich blackland area of pecan and cotton, abstinence and Jesus. According to its Bulletin,

> Southwestern, being an Assemblies of God school, embraces standards of living and conduct that are the same as those generally accepted by the Pentecostal churches in America. These are characterized by clean conduct and conversation, modest apparel in dress, high standards of moral life, and a deep consecration and devotion in spiritual life. . . . Most certainly will the relationship between sexes reflect moral purity as well as a distaste for promiscuity.

It was here, to this place, that Jerry Lee Lewis came, traveling by bus some four hundred miles, to start life over on the eve of his fifteenth birthday. He looked around him, saw the tan brick buildings, the sparse trees, and the stained-glass chapel from which no sound came. He looked around and saw the young men and women smiling to one another in Christian earnest. He looked around and longed for Haney's Big House.

Most of those attending Southwestern were college students who took courses like Introduction to Missions, Pentecostal Truth, Major Prophets, Elementary Accounting, Exegesis of Isaiah, and Church Business; but many, like Jerry Lee, were enrolled in the Junior College Division. While Jerry Lee was, in his way, an ardent student of the Bible, he found classes here to be no more bearable than they had been at Ferriday High.

Soon he took to creeping out at night, crawling from his dormitory window while his classmates slept. There was not much to do in Waxahachie at night. It was a town of not many more than 8,000 souls, and the majority of those had been saved. There were no nightclubs, no unbuttoned women, no anything as far as Jerry Lee could tell. But lo! some thirty miles north on Highway 75, there she lay with lifted skirt and liquored breath, all flashing lights and fury: Dallas.

He would hitchhike to Dallas and go to the picture shows. He would sneak into nightclubs and hear the bands. He would go to the amusement park, get on the Tilt-a-Whirl, and tell the cowboy who ran it to turn the sucker wide open and let it rip, and he would spin faster and faster, endlessly, feeling all that was within him contract and rise in fluttering escape like a sudden shot of neon from his lungs—like magic.

Jerry Lee lingered at the Bible Institute for about three months, skipping classes and sneaking to Dallas. He was called upon one evening to play piano at chapel service, which he gladly did. But when he began playing the Pentecostal hymn "My God Is Real," the preacher shot him a glance of reproach, for he was playing it boogie-woogie style, and he was playing it faster and faster until it was double tempo, and then an unseen student in the congregation gave a joyous howl, and then there was another, and Jerry Lee heard both of these howls, and he beat the boogie so hard that there was nothing left of the hymn, nothing but the sounds of the Holy Ghost that had inspired it, and he cried out the final lyric and raked the keys violently back and forth.

My God is real, for I can feel Him in my soul!

He was grinning and breathing hard. And then he was expelled from Southwestern Bible Institute. Before leaving Waxahachie, he said what was on his mind to all who would listen. He said, "You can't get the Bible from all these silly books y'all got here." Then he boarded the bus and returned to Ferriday.

Six

Mamie Lewis was disappointed, but she was glad to have her son home again. Every morning she brought him breakfast in bed on an old tray that she dressed with tinfoil: hot chocolate and Jack's Vanilla Wafers. She sat by him with her own hot chocolate and her own Jack's Vanilla Wafers. Neither of them would accept any other make of vanilla cookie. "Jack's cookies are always smiling fresh!" declared the man in the radio advertisement, and both Jerry Lee and his mama knew this to be true.

Mamie's parents were living in the house now. Her mother, Theresa Lee, had lost her mind. She spoke to the walls—gave them names, bore grudges against them, cast demons from them, and threatened them with eternal damnation. She had little truck with the people around her, children and grandchildren. It was between her and the walls. Her husband, J.W., who was now in his eighties, sat by her and tried to correct her, reprimand her, as if it were all a matter of misbe-havior. "Girl," he would say, "enough." Then he would shake his head and recede into that other century whence he had come.

"It run in her family," the doctor told Elmo. "It run in her blood."

Old Theresa Lee frightened some of her younger kin, but her son-in-law Elmo would have no talk of sending her away, for things simply were not done that way. "Someday y'all might be in-sane, too," he would say. Her other son-in-law, Lee Calhoun, always patted her on the head and asked her how she was feeling. She seemed to like him and treated him al-most like a wall.

In the summer of 1951, Ferriday's main thoroughfare, Fourth Street, was paved. This same summer Jerry Lee met a seventeen-year-old girl named Dorothy Barton, a pretty girl with high, strong cheekbones and thick, dark, wavy hair. She was the daughter of Reverend Jewell E. Barton, a Pentecostal preacher from the town of Sterlington, near Monroe. A few months later, in February, 1952, when Jerry Lee was sixteen, he and Dorothy went to the Concordia Parish Court House in Vidalia and applied for a marriage license. Jerry Lee lied about most of the information asked of him, while Dorothy did not.

> Name: Jerry Lewis
> Usual Residence: Sterlington, Union Parish
> Date of Birth: Sept. 29, 1930
> Last Grade of School Completed: 8th
> Present Occupation: Farmer
>
> Name: Dorothy Barton
> Usual Residence: Sterlington, Union Parish
> Date of Birth: Nov. 10, 1933
> Last Grade of School Completed: 11th

They were married by Reverend W. W. Hall in Lee Calhoun's house on Louisiana Avenue on February 21. A photographer from the *Concordia Sentinel* came to the house and took pictures of the couple, and the pictures were published the following month in the column "Ferriday Happenings." Jerry Lee was grinning, slightly, crookedly, staring at God knows what, his blond hair combed back in thick waves, his ears still sticking out, but not so much as they had in childhood.

Dorothy moved in with the Lewis family out near Black River. Jerry Lee was talking a great deal about becoming a minister. He even took to composing sermons. Elmo had made a pinewood mantel for the fireplace, but he had never gotten around to staining it. Jerry Lee paced throughout the little house, working up sermons in his head. Whenever something truly fine came to him—words of eternal damnation, words of wonder—he went to the mantel and began to scrawl. As the weeks passed, the homely pine-board mantel was filled with exhortations, allusions to the Pentateuch, and the blood of Christ. In its planed, knotted grain were serpents and the sins of the Israelites.

Jerry Lee spoke to the minister of the Church of God on Mississippi Avenue, and the minister told him that he was welcome to preach. On several Sundays during the last warm days of the year, Jerry Lee took the pulpit in the little white three-eaved Church of God. He raised his voice and preached about the rich man in hell—how that rich man cried out to Abraham for a drop of water to cool his dry tongue, and how Abraham gave him none, for no man can serve God and Mammon both. Jerry Lee told it to them, and he told it right. People congratulated him, told him that he had the makings of a great preacher, that he *was* a great preacher.

But Jerry Lee ceased writing on the mantel, and he ceased to preach. He let his marriage to Dorothy fall to the ground, too.

He began to run out into the night, leaving Dorothy at home with his mother and sisters. One evening everyone was sitting in the yard, eating watermelon, spitting out the pits, not speaking. Jerry Lee's friend Cecil Harrelson came by, and he and Jerry went into the house. When they came out Jerry Lee was wearing a white sports coat, and he was wet-combing his hair as he walked.

"Me and Cecil are goin' out," he announced from the side of his mouth. Dorothy's forehead tightened and she spat a pit to the dirt.

"No," Mamie said. "You're married now, and it ain't right the way you do, goin' out on the town every night." Her eyes were clear and cutting.

"Me and Cecil are goin' out," he said, looking at neither his wife nor his mother, but at Cecil's beat-up Ford.

"Oh, really?" Mamie said.

"Yeah, really," Jerry Lee said.

Mamie took her hunk of dripping red watermelon and hurled it at her son, and it smashed against his breast, all over that fancy white jacket. Jerry Lee turned and reentered the house. He came back out wearing a different jacket, one Aunt Stella had given him. He strode to Cecil's car and rode away into the warm dusk.

By the spring of 1953, Dorothy had left him and returned to her family. Much else had changed, too. Jimmy Swaggart was married to a wonderful girl who spoke in tongues. They lived together in a small trailer parked in Irene Gilley's front yard. On Saturdays Jimmy Lee roamed from town to town, preaching on street corners, explaining how America was thigh-deep in sin and under the judgment of God. He carried with him an accordion, and he sang "There Is Power in the Blood," and he collected what coin he could. He even preached as far as Mangham, whence his forebears' seed had blown. After he had preached in enough of these towns, he built up the courage to start preaching in the streets of Ferriday, where all knew him.

One night Jimmy Lee could not sleep. He left his trailer and walked in darkness. When he returned, just before dawn, he found a hideous creature awaiting him. This creature had the form of a great bear and the visage of a man, and its eyes were the yellow of evils unimagined.

"In the name of Jeeesus!" Jimmy Lee hollered.

Upon hearing the name of the Lord, the creature fell to the ground and writhed, baying in agony.

"In the name of Jeeeeeesus!" Jimmy Lee hollered.

The creature crept away, twisting and groaning and clutching itself. Jimmy Lee lifted his hands to God and spoke in an unknown tongue. Then he entered the bed where his wife, Frances, slept, and he embraced her, and he closed his eyes in strength and in peace, and he slept.

Mickey Gilley, too, was married now, living in Houston, running a ditching machine for his father-in-law's construction company. He no longer spoke in tongues, and little by little the old ways left him.

After his marriage ended, Jerry Lee threw himself deep into his music. Though he was still a minor, he began to seek nightclub work. His friend Cecil served as a sort of manager. Together they rode to New Orleans, then Monroe, where Jerry Lee made some money playing piano with the house band at the Little Club, a bucket of blood on the outskirts of town. It was a country band, with a steel-player and a fiddler. The guitarist was crippled and sometimes painful to watch. One night as the band was playing, a large man with rolled-up sleeves walked into the Little Club. He drank six shots of whiskey, then asked if he could play the fiddle awhile. The fiddler handed him his instrument and bow, and the large man commenced to make with that instrument and bow a series of harsh screeching sounds, tapping rhythm with his foot as the band played behind him. The large man turned out to be Otis Brown, and he was the son of Elmo's younger sister Jane. He and Jerry Lee were first cousins. Someday, by means of some fancy Chinee arithmetic, they would be uncle and nephew as well.

Jerry Lee also played, as a solo act, in the Domino Lounge at the Alvis Hotel on the corner of DeSiard and North Fifth, in the vicinity of forgotten Lewiston. The man who ran the Domino Lounge was reluctant to hire Jerry Lee, but Cecil spoke up for his friend.

"I got a boy here," he said, "who can play a piano better'n anything you ever heard."

"Get the hell out of here," the man said.

"Just give me a chance," Jerry Lee said. "Just give me a chance is all I want."

"Boy, you got one chance," the man said, "and if you can't play that piano, I'm gonna kick your goddamn ass up between your shoulders."

Jerry Lee played "Down Yonder," an old song that he had learned from a 1951 record by a lady piano player named Del Wood. The man hired him. By the time Jerry Lee quit the Domino Lounge, he had made more than two hundred dollars in tips. When he came home to Ferriday, he showed the money to his mother.

"My God, Elmo!" she cried. "He broke into a store!"

By the summer of 1953, Jerry Lee had begun to work in the clubs along Highway 61 North on the outskirts of Natchez, Mississippi: the 61 Club, the Hilltop Club, the Dixie Club. These were wide-open saloons frequented by gamblers, whores, and drunkards. Jerry Lee played most often at the Dixie Club. Since this club was raided with great regularity,

and since Jerry Lee was still a minor, the owner installed a little door in the wall behind the bandstand. Whenever the bar-
maid up front gave the signal that the cops had arrived, Jerry
Lee scurried through his door and waited outside in the bushes
till the joint was clear.

In Natchez Jerry Lee discovered Nellie Jackson's, which
throughout his life he would extol as "the greatest whorehouse
in the South." Miss Nellie was a black woman, the daughter of
freed slaves. She never told anyone her age, but it was a known
fact around Natchez that she had been running a whorehouse
in the same location since at least 1935. Four-sixteen North
Rankin Street did not look like much from the outside: a few
stone steps leading to a high, fortresslike fence made of uneven
wooden planks; set into the fence at the top of the stone steps
was a heavy plank door; beyond the door was a grown-over
path leading to the rear entrance of an old house; and up these
stairs, on the second floor: Miss Nellie's. Inside Miss Nellie's
the music never ceased, the liquor never stopped flowing, and
the girls—white girls, black girls—never quit crossing and
uncrossing their legs in a way that showed you that they wore
no drawers beneath their little nighties. There was a jukebox,
a piano, a table, and a bar, and over the door there was a man's
wooden leg, with the shoe and sock still on, hanging there by
one of its army-green straps. Its owner had tried to get something for nothing, and Miss Nellie's girls had ripped that
thing from his knee, hinges and all. Off from this entertain-
ment room there were several bedrooms. One of these bedrooms contained the first circular bed in the state of
Mississippi. Another was Miss Nellie's room, where she slept
and drank and played with her poodles. It was to this place on
North Rankin Street that young Jerry Lee came, to laugh and
to disgorge himself in the pale, passive flesh of those women
within whom the Holy Ghost did not abide. Occasionally Miss

Nellie would visit one of the clubs out on Highway 61 and loudly applaud for Jerry Lee. She never forgot him, remembering him always as "that Ferriday music man."

It was also in Natchez, in the summer of 1953, that Jerry Lee met a seventeen-year-old girl named Jane Mitcham, who lived with her mother, Sallie, over on North Pine Street. They met at a roller-skating rink, and they lay together. About a month before Jerry Lee's eighteenth birthday Jane told him that his seed had taken hold within her, and that he must wed her. He explained to her that he had never bothered to divorce his first wife, that in the eyes of God and the sovereign state of Louisiana he was still married to Dorothy. Violently cursing, violently crying, Jane departed from him.

Frankie Jean recalls that, a few days later, several of Jane's brothers arrived in Ferriday bearing horsewhips and pistols. They did not find Jerry Lee, but they did encounter Lee Calhoun. They told Uncle Lee that their sister had been wronged and now Jerry Lee must marry her. Two of the Mitcham boys did not want Jerry Lee to marry their sister; they simply wanted to release his soul. Uncle Lee dealt with these two first, and then he dealt with the others, and then he brought them all together with Elmo and Jerry Lee, and they all did some arithmeticking. And while Uncle Lee may have saved his nephew's life, he was not able to save him from marriage.

Jerry Lee and Jane entered the Natchez Court House just a few minutes before it closed for the day, September 10. He gave his age as twenty-one and his address as that of Jane's mother. Five days later they went to the town of Fayette, about twenty miles north of Natchez, and there they were married. He had become a bigamist at the tender age of seventeen.

Jerry Lee and his new bride moved into a garage apartment on Louisiana Avenue in downtown Ferriday. From the very beginning, Jane tried to get Jerry Lee to quit the clubs and settle down. After all, she explained, he was going to be a father. At the end of 1953 (after belatedly divorcing his first wife, on October 8, in Monroe), he took a job working on the pipeline. This lasted three days. Then he became a salesman for a sewing machine company. He and another boy roamed through south Louisiana in a 1947 Pontiac that Jerry Lee had acquired. Cruising along, Jerry Lee had him one of his fine ideas. He shared this idea with his fellow employee, and the fellow employee agreed that it was indeed a fine idea; so they executed it.

They went about their business, lugging their sales model sewing machine from door to door. Jerry Lee sold hell out of those machines, but he was sometimes slow in delivering the down payments to the company. This went on for quite a while. Then one day Jerry Lee and his fellow employee stopped for a Coke and a game of pool at one of those old country stores set way off from any town. In the cracked glass case below the cash register, Jerry Lee noticed a big blue-steel .45 revolver. He didn't even ask the old bastard how much the gun cost; he just paid for the Coke and left. This was in the afternoon. Sometime after midnight Jerry Lee and his fellow employee returned to the darkened store, hammered open the door, and took the big blue-steel .45 out of its case. They got back into the 1947 Pontiac and drove off. They were laughing, playing with the gun, and they didn't see the black-and-white car coming up behind them until it was too late.

They were locked up in jail for the night, then for another night. Then they were brought before a judge. The judge addressed Jerry Lee and his partner, and with a voice of great compassion he sentenced them both to two years in prison. The traveling sales team regarded one another and breathed loudly. The young lawyer who had been defending the boys, with great deference and obsequiousness to the judge, and

Seven

It was at the Dixie Club that Jerry Lee met Johnny Littlejohn. Born upstate in Tupelo, in 1924, Johnny at this time was a disc jockey at WNAT in Natchez. Besides broadcasting his daily show from the Eola Hotel, Johnny was also the leader of a band that worked in various dives around town.

Jerry Lee joined Johnny Littlejohn's band in 1954, the year that the Hilltop Club was struck by what certain folks in Natchez referred to as Jewish lightning. After the Hilltop Club burned down, its owner, Julius A. May, purchased the Dixie Club and renamed it the Wagon Wheel.

Johnny Littlejohn's band played at the Wagon Wheel most every night. Johnny played bass, switching to drums after the band's original drummer was locked up for nonsupport. Joe Jones played steel guitar. A fifty-year-old blind man named Paul Whitehead played electric accordion, trumpet, and piano. Jerry Lee started out as the band's drummer, with Littlejohn returning to the bass. Slowly Jerry Lee took over at the piano, and Littlejohn ended up once again at the drums.

The band played from eight o'clock at night till whenever the joint closed, which might be anytime between two and four the following morning. Whatever money they made was divided equally. This usually came out to about ten dollars a night for each of them. On weekends, when Tex Reed joined the band on tenor sax, they made more.

The music was a perverse mixture of country and blues and pop songs. "We played everything, man," Johnny Littlejohn recalled a quarter of a century later, after the Wagon Wheel had been reduced to emptiness and Mississippi wind. "We played everything from 'The Wild Side of Life' and 'Slippin' Around' to 'Big Legged Woman' and 'Drinkin' Wine, Spo-Dee-O-Dee.' Hell, we did 'Stardust.' We just played it all. Whatever we did, we did it honky-tonk style, hard-core barroom style. Paul Whitehead made that electric accordion sound like a damn brass section. A guy came into the club one New Year's Eve when we were playin', and he thought it was a nigger band. Hell, man, we just did it—we played it all.

"Whenever Jerry sang he could never remember the words to anything. I'd feed him the words. He'd be sittin' there at the piano and I'd be sittin' right near him at the drums, and I'd feed him the lyrics as he was singin'. Hell, he couldn't even remember the words to 'Slippin' Around,' and there ain't but a dozen of 'em. But he was somethin' to see, man. He was always a showman. Always."

In the summer of 1954 began the greatest revolution in the history of the music business since the invention of sound-recording: whitefolk rock 'n' roll. What black men had been doing since the mid-forties was now recast by a handful of young white boys who had spent their youth hearing those black men, falling under the spell of their magic, learning. Now they recast that magic, mixed it with white magic, and gave forth something that had not been heard before. They called it rock 'n' roll, the same phrase that blacks had been using for more than a decade; but they let the white people who bought it think that they had invented the phrase, as they let them think that they had invented the music. This, too, they had learned from those black men.

One could see the beginnings of this revolution by looking at the August 7, 1954, issue of the music-business trade weekly *Billboard*. On one page there was an advertisement for the new Bill Haley record, "Shake, Rattle and Roll" (an expurgated version of the Joe Turner original which had been released less than three months before). Here, for the first time, Bill Haley & His Comets were being marketed as "The Nation's 'Rockingest' Rhythm Group." A few pages later, in the "Reviews of New C&W Records," there was a review of a record by a young Southern man released by Trumpet, a small Mississippi label: "Gonna Roll and Rock" by Lucky Joe Almond. ("He sings it pleasantly, if unimpressively," the reviewer remarked.) But on the opposite page was a much more favorable review of another new record, also by a young Southern man and also released by a small Southern label. It was a review of Elvis Presley's first record, cut at the Sun Studio in Memphis the previous month, and it was the first mention of Elvis in a national publication. "Presley is a potent new chanter," the anonymous reviewer said, "who can sock over a tune for either the country or the r.&b. markets. On this new disk he comes through with a solid performance on an r.&b.-type tune ['That's All Right'] and then on the flip side does another fine job with a country ditty ['Blue Moon of Kentucky']. A strong new talent." Onward from this hot, glistering August, rock 'n' roll endlessly came.

On November 2, a little more than a month after his nineteenth birthday (and a little more than thirteen months after his shotgun wedding), Jerry Lee became a father. He named the boy Jerry Lee Lewis, Jr. Following the birth of his son, Jerry Lee made two journeys, searching for unbuttoned fame. The first of these journeys was to Shreveport, where he auditioned for "The Louisiana Hayride," the KWKH Saturday-night radio show that had given Hank Williams his start and on which just a few weeks before, on October 16, Elvis Presley had performed.

"Horace Logan was runnin' the 'Hayride' at the time, wearin' little ol' cap pistols and shit like that. Thought he was a kingpin," Jerry Lee recalled of his trip to Shreveport. "I begged him to let me do a number onstage. He kept stallin' and stallin', and then finally he says, 'I tell you what, son, you can audition for Slim Whitman.' Logan says he don't remember, but he does. He's a liar."

Slim Whitman was a languid thirty-year-old country singer who had been at the fore of "The Louisiana Hayride" since April, 1950. He set Jerry Lee at a piano in the KWKH studio and had a technician make an acetate disc recording of him. The two songs that Jerry Lee chose to audition with were both Number One hits: "I Don't Hurt Anymore," which was currently on the country charts by Hank Snow, and "I Need You Now," which had first been recorded, the previous year, by pop singer Joni James and was now a pop hit by Eddie Fisher. Though the sound-quality of these KWKH recordings was primitive, the strength and maturity of his voice were unmistakable. He performed both songs similarly, playing melody as he sang, then filling in the spaces between the lyrics with hard honky-tonk licks. Slim Whitman listened to the disc, then handed it to Jerry Lee, saying, "Don't call me, I'll call you."

Jerry Lee's second journey was to Nashville. He checked

into a dollar-a-night room at the Bell Hotel, across from the Continental Bus depot. He walked up and down Sixteenth and Seventeenth Avenues South with that acetate disc under his arm, feeling for all the world like Christopher Columbus and his ball. He snuck backstage at the Ryman Auditorium during the Saturday night "Opry" show. Gaunt, sallow men in rhinestone suits and white Stetsons pushed past him to and from the stage. Two women, both "Opry" regulars, befriended him: Del Wood, the lady who had recorded "Down Yonder," and Goldie Hill, a pretty, blond singer who was only a few years older than he.

Jerry Lee found brief employment at the Musicians' Hideaway, an upstairs after-hours joint at 55 Commerce Street, around the corner from the hotel he was staying at. Roy Hall, the owner of the club, was a hard-drinking piano player from Big Stone Gap, Virginia, about twenty miles north of the Tennessee line.

"I hired him," Hall later recalled, "for fifteen dollars a night. He worked from one till five in the mornin', poundin' that damn piano till daylight. Folks would give Jerry Lee their watches and jewelry, in case there was a bust, figurin' that he'd be the one that was let off, y'know, on account of his age. We had blackjack goin', roulette, everything. The night we got raided, Jerry Lee had about fifteen wristwatches on his arms. They took everybody to the station, locked 'em up. Sure enough, the only one they didn't frisk was Jerry Lee. I put up a bond and got everybody out, and they all got their watches and stuff back. We just went right back to the club and opened up again."

Not long after the bust, Jerry Lee quit the Musicians' Hideaway and returned his attention to auditioning for record companies. When his money began to run out, he wired Uncle Lee and Aunt Stella, and they sent him twenty-five dollars. He continued to knock on record company doors until the twenty-five dollars were spent. But wherever he went it was the same.

"They said, 'Well, now, you change your act to a gittar and you might could make it.' I said, 'You can take your gittar and ram it up your ass.' I hitchhiked back to Natchez, Mississippi, and went to work again at the Wagon Wheel."

Back home, things were not good between him and Jane. She threatened to leave him if he did not quit his nighttime ways. She damned the Wagon Wheel, and she damned his piano, and she damned his soul. He excoriated her for drinking and smoking and for other sins against the Holy Ghost; and he accused her of adultery.

He used his little sister Linda Gail as a spy. "I would go off to town with Jerry's wife and my sister and I would bribe them," recounted Linda Gail. "I was about seven or eight years old, and I'd say, 'If you give me a cigarette and a drink of your beer, I won't tell Jerry on you.' You see, Jerry would not allow what they were doing and I knew this. So they would give me everything and I'd promise them the world and give them nothing. As soon as I got home, I'd climb up on Jerry's lap and he'd say, 'Well, Linda, tell me what they did.' Then I would proceed to tell everything on them. I was always Jerry's pet."

"Jane was something," Frankie Jean Lewis remembered. "They were fighting one night when Mother was there, and Mother got dragged into it. Jerry Lee decided to walk out in the middle of everything. Mother slapped him and he ducked and she broke her finger against the wall. Jane would always rely on Mother to help control Jerry. Which Mother always did, but she never could keep him from going out. I don't think she really wanted to."

Not all of Jerry Lee's fights were with his wife. There were struggles with a demon. "He was tortured," Johnny Littlejohn said. "He was torn between music and that Assembly of God. He'd get into that thing about God and Mammon, get on that preacher kick. I'd drive over to Ferriday to get him and he'd tell me he was gonna be a preacher. 'I ain't gonna play in no more clubs. I'm gonna live for the Lord,' he'd say. I'd beg him to come. Sometimes he would, sometimes he wouldn't. Once he stayed away for two full weeks, then he called me and said, 'Well, John, y'know, things are gettin' bad and I need the bread.'"

In February, 1955, Jane told Jerry Lee that she must go to Hazlehurst, Mississippi, where her grandfather was dying. Not long after she left, Jerry Lee found her in a store in nearby Jonesville. He told her to gather her worldly goods from their apartment and leave. He told her that he would no longer have her; he called her a liar and a whore.

She went to Monroe, to the home of her older sister. In Monroe she sued Jerry Lee for divorce, and a judge awarded her forty dollars a month. Jerry Lee did not agree with this judge, and he did not give her forty dollars—not that month, not the month after that—and Jane had him arrested by court order. Then, in June, she dropped her suit and she returned to Ferriday, to her husband and her baby child. She caressed Jerry Lee and soon told him that she was pregnant. He told her that it was no seed of his that had rendered her so. They lifted their hands in anger anew.

"I'd go over there to pick him up sometimes," said Johnny Littlejohn of those summer nights of 1955, "and he'd come down the stairs. Lamps'd foller 'im, pots an' pans, every damn thing else. That ol' lady of his, that Jane, she was a tiger. One night she come out to the club. She stood outside, and he wouldn't go out to see her. She took one of her nasty ol' high-heel shoes and she went at that '47 Pontiac of his—bashed out every damn piece of glass in that sonofabitch." But the weaker vessel could never stop the music—no, only the Holy Ghost could do that—and it went on. Night after night, it went on.

As wild a place as the Wagon Wheel was, there were joints in Natchez that were wilder by far. These were found on the Mississippi riverfront, along a small stretch of lowland beneath a bluff. Since before the Civil War this area had been known as Under-the-Hill. It was here that the keelboats, then later the steamboats, had docked, and it was here, old-timers said, on this little postage stamp of waterfront, that more drinking, gambling, fucking, and killing had been done than anywhere else in the entire grand and goddamn state of Mississippi.

"Natchez under the Hill—where, oh! where shall I find words suitable to describe the peculiarities of this unholy spot?" quavered the author of the *Life of Davy Crockett* in 1860. " 'Tis, in fact, the jumping off place. Satan looks on it with glee, and chuckles as he beholds the orgies of his votaries. The buildings are for the most part brothels, taverns, or gambling houses, and frequently the whole may be found under the same roof. Obscene songs are sung at the top of the voice in all quarters. I have repeatedly seen the strumpets tear a man's clothes from his back and leave his body beautified with all the colors of the rainbow."

Ninety-five years later, Under-the-Hill was still a place that Satan might look on with glee. Bars like the Canasta Club and Toney Marsella's Blue Cat Club were places where a man or a woman could drink, gamble, kill or be killed. In 1955 Johnny Littlejohn's band, with Jerry Lee and blind old Paul Whitehead, became the Blue Cat Club's most popular band. Unlike the Wagon Wheel, the Blue Cat Club sometimes did not close till way past that bright and busying hour when decent folks had eaten breakfast and started off to work.

One night Elmo and Mamie, Frankie Jean and little Linda

Gail drove across the bridge to Natchez to see just what sort of place Jerry Lee was working at. Elmo parked the car along the dirt road that separated the Blue Cat Club from the Mississippi River. They heard a harrowing din that rose and fell but never ceased.

"Mother was so frightened," Frankie Jean said of that night. "She kept sayin', 'Oh, God, they're gonna kill us all, they're gonna kill us all. Oh, my God, my son, my son.' It was a terrible place. And Jerry was in there bangin' away. You could hear him all the way outside, cuttin' through that wicked racket with his piano. Daddy went inside; the rest of us waited in the car with the doors locked and the windows rolled up."

Elmo walked past the crowded bar, past the roulette wheel, the blackjack table, and the Beat-My-Shake—walked until he saw his son, sitting up there at the piano, pounding and howling about how them big-legged women better keep their dresses down 'cause when he started drillin' on 'em they were gonna lose their nightgowns, and that old blind man standing up there next to him, nodding his head up and down and wrenching at that electric squeeze-box as if it were the instrument of his blindness and he could not free himself from it. Elmo liked it—all of it. He had him a drink, and he liked it even more.

The band was never at a loss for new material, since Johnny Littlejohn, as a WNAT disc jockey, received copies of all the new records, blues, country, and pop. One of the new releases that came through the mail during the first week of October, 1955, Jerry Lee took a special liking to: "Whole Lotta Shakin' Goin' On," a Decca record by Roy Hall, the fellow who had hired Jerry Lee to work in his after-hours joint in Nashville several months before.

Roy Hall was thirty-three years old and playing piano in country singer Webb Pierce's band when he cut "Whole Lotta

Shakin' Goin' On," in September, 1955. It was his first record for Decca. Before then he had recorded for Fortune Records in Detroit, as Roy Hall and His Cohutta Mountain Boys, and for the Nashville companies Tennessee and Bullet, and was best known for his song "The Dirty Boogie." Though Hall was a powerful pianist, there was no piano on his recording of "Whole Lotta Shakin' Goin' On," and most of the record's hard-edged drive came from the burly licks of Sugarfoot Garland's electric guitar. There was a blurred, drunken tone in Roy Hall's voice as he sang.

> *Twenty-one drums and an ol' bass horn,*
> *Somebody beatin' on a ding-dong.*
> *Come on over, baby, whole lotta shakin' goin'*
> *   on;*
> *Come on over, baby; baby, you can't go wrong.*
>
> *There ain't no fakin', whole lotta shakin' goin'*
> *   on.*
> *Come on over, baby, whole lotta kickin' in the*
> *   barn;*
> *Come on over, baby, we got the bull by the*
> *   horns;*
> *Well, there ain't no fakin', whole lotta shakin'*
> *   goin' on.*
>
> *Shake, make it shake. Shake, make it shake.*
> *Shake, don't let it break. Shake, an' make it*
> *   shake.*
> *There ain't no fakin', whole lotta shakin' goin'*
> *   on.*

"Me an' a black guy by the name of Dave Williams put it together," Roy Hall said. "We was down at Pahokee, Florida, out at Lake Okeechobee. We was drunk, writin' songs. We was out there fishin' an' milkin' snakes, drinkin' wine. This guy had a big bell out there an' he'd ring it to get us all to come in to dinner. An' I call over there to the other part of the island—I say, 'What's goin' on?' Black guy said, 'We got twenty-one drums'—see, they's all drunk—'We got an ol' bass horn an' they even keepin' time on a ding-dong.' See, that's the big bell they'd ring to get us to come in." ("Beatin' on the Ding Dong" was also the title of a record that country singer Jim Reeves had released in May, 1954.)

"When me an' Curly Williams copyrighted the song, I used a pen name, Sunny David. I had me a lotta pen names. Shady Walls—that was one of 'em. See, I's tryin' to get away from that income tax. They finally caught my ass, too. I still get a little bit from the royalties, but not much. I lost out in a lawsuit to my ex-wife. An' Paul Cohen, who was the head of Decca, he got me to sign a buncha papers when I's drunk, an' I lost a lot that way. One of them kinda deals. But I don't drink no more—quit in '72."

Though Roy Hall was the song's co-author, he was not the first to record it. The mighty R & B singer Big Maybelle had cut it the previous March for Okeh Records in New York. Like Big Maybelle's record, Roy Hall's was not a hit; but it did inspire a couple of flip-side cover versions. Within a month of Hall's recording, the song was done by another Decca act—big-band singer Dolores Fredericks—and in late December Dot Records in Nashville released a version by the Commodores, a pop vocal group.

But "Jerry Lee liked the hell outa that damn record," Johnny Littlejohn recalled. "He kept sayin', 'Lemme sing it.' I said, 'You don't know the words, Jerry Lee.' He said, 'Well, you can feed 'em to me.' And I fed 'em to him, and he sang the fire outa that sucker."

Neither Johnny nor Jerry Lee himself knew that in this little song Jerry Lee had found his dirt: dirt upon which would rise a tale wilder and darker, bigger and badder, than any lived, told, or even dreamed by those who came before—a tale whose trailing, darkling embers would sting the very eyes of the Holy Ghost before falling, alighting, sinking, returning in quiet mystery to the Louisiana bottomland.⌋

And Jerry Lee by now had found something else, too— something that in time would hew and cut the brow and fist of the tale. He had been taught more than new songs and fed more than words. There were fifteen-milligram Benzedrine capsules—little magic pills.

Eight

On the day after Christmas, 1955, Jerry Lee's grandmother Theresa Lee Herron passed on to her myriad-walled reward. Her husband, J.W., had died the previous spring, and now they laid her beside him and covered her with Calhoun dirt in the little cemetery near Clayton.

Ten weeks later, on March 16, there was new life. Jane gave birth to a second son, and she named him Ronnie Guy, after her father. But Jerry Lee saw that the child's hair was darker than his own, and he declared to his wife that it was no son of his, and that it would never, even unto its tenth generation, enter the kingdom of God.

That summer, Mickey Gilley, who was still working for the Smith Construction Company in Houston, drove into Ferriday to visit his people. He encountered Jerry Lee walking down a street, and Jerry Lee told him about the band he was playing in and about the Blue Cat Club. Both cousins had been seeing a lot of stories about Elvis lately in magazines like *Rock and Roll Songs, Country Song Roundup,* and *Country & Western Jamboree*— stories with titles such as "Elvis Presley—Skyrocket to Fame."

"Jerry, why don't you go to Memphis, *Tennessee,*" Mickey said, "and talk to the guy that started Elvis."

"I'll do that one of these days," Jerry Lee said, looking away to the side.

Jerry Lee talked to his father about this, and Elmo agreed that it was a good idea, especially seeing as Jerry Lee was now twenty-one years old and did not know how to do a damn thing but make music and get his ass in trouble. That fall Elmo pumped almost four hundred eggs from his hens, and he and Jerry Lee took those eggs, those thirty-three dozen eggs, and sold them to Nelson's Supermarket on Louisiana Avenue. What Nelson's wouldn't have they sold to a little grocery store in Jonesville. Elmo put the egg money away and he waited.

On a Saturday night in November, the night after Jerry Lee, Jr.'s second birthday, Jerry Lee took Johnny Littlejohn aside at the Blue Cat Club.

"John," he said, "this is gonna be my last night."

"Oh, hell, not again," Johhny Littlejohn said. "What is it? You're gonna be a preacher?"

"No," Jerry Lee said. "I'm goin' to Memphis. I'm gonna cut me a record. If I don't make it, I'll never hit another lick as long as I live."

Johnny blew Lucky smoke from his nostrils and nodded, making like he understood.

The next morning, Jerry Lee and Elmo took the egg money, plus twenty dollars that Jerry Lee had made at the club that week, and they got in Jerry Lee's new Ford and headed north on Highway 65. It was raining, and dark all the way.

Nine

Sam Phillips had got into the record business by way of radio. Born on a farm near Florence, Alabama, on January 5, 1923, he began working as a radio announcer at WLAY in Muscle Shoals in 1941. From there he went to WHSL in Decatur, then to WLAC in Nashville. In the winter of 1944–45, he came to WREC in Memphis, where he produced live broadcasts of swing bands from the Hotel Peabody. With the money he made, he built a small studio in a converted radiator shop at 706 Union Avenue, and in 1950 he began recording black musicians and leasing these recordings to independent labels such as Chess, Modern, Meteor, and Trumpet. He recorded some of the best bluesmen in the South: Bobby Bland, Little Milton, James Cotton, Howlin' Wolf, B. B. King, Ike Turner, Joe Hill Louis, and others who had been scuffling around in a thousand places like Haney's Big House. Early in 1952 Sam started his own record company. Sun Records began

Thunder without rain.

as a blues label, with scattered hillbilly releases. Then, in the summer of 1954, along came Elvis, and Sun was soon no longer a blues label, but instead the premier label of whitefolk rock 'n' roll. Toward the end of 1955, Sam let Elvis go to RCA-Victor for $40,000, which at that time was an unheard-of sum in the record business. Since then there had been other successful Sun artists—Carl Perkins, Johnny Cash—but Sam had not found another Elvis.

During that rainy ride to Memphis, Jerry Lee and Elmo talked about what they would say to Mr. Phillips, about what songs Jerry Lee should perform for him. They arrived in Memphis at dusk and found a room at a downtown hotel for a dollar fifty a night. In the morning they asked directions and started walking toward Sun Records and all imagined things. When they walked into 706 Union Avenue, they were told by the receptionist that Sam Phillips had left for Nashville earlier that morning to attend the fifth annual D.J. Convention and that there was no one in the studio but herself and Jack Clement, a producer.

Many years later, after the hotel had been torn down and Sun boarded up, Jerry Lee and Elmo sat drinking whiskey, talking about that day, to each other more than to those around them.

"We slept together that first night in Memphis, *Ten*nessee. That was the first time an' the las' time," Elmo said, now in his seventies, still smiling, but slurring now, too.

"Yeah," his son, the final wild son, said, not smiling now any more than he ever had, "in a little ol' room with a little ol' bed in it. There was a sink in there, an' that looked like a million dollars. Runnin' water. That meant a lot, didn't it?"

"Shoot, you talkin' 'bout *run*nin' water? Didn't have none back home—hadda go out an' pump."

"Dollar an' a half. I swear to God, I ain't seen that hotel since. I looked, but I can't find it."

"Next mornin' I ask the man, I says, 'Where's Sun Records at?' He says, 'It's right down the street.' We sat around there, then finally that, that Clement—Jack Clement was his name, I believe—"

"That sonofabitch."

"We sat around," Elmo continued, "till 'bout one, two o'clock, waitin' that woman."

"Yeah, that pig."

"She was a good ol' girl."

"She was a shit. 'Xcuse m'language."

"Anyway, uh, we waited and waited. I done the talkin'—"

"Who done the what?"

"I done the talkin'."

"I b'lieve I'm gonna have t'argue with ya there, Pappy."

"I talked like hell."

"I know you talked."

"Damn right I talked."

"But I did throw in a few important—"

"I know you did—"

"I told 'em, *'I'm* gonna be heard by Sam Phillips if I have to set on his damn doorstep till he comes back.'"

"That's right, you did."

"Jack, he taped it down. See, he knew what he was doin'. I couldn't see it then, but I can see it now."

"That woman says, 'This boy here wants to audition.' This *boy* wants to audition. Shoot."

"That bitch."

"Says, 'Where's your gittar?' Says, 'I don't play no gittar, I play a piana.' Says, 'There's a piana—go on.' He had some tape hangin' there on a nail on the wall."

"Naw, he didn't say that at first. He didn't wanna let us

in—said, 'Son, I ain't got time t'fool with ya.' That's what he said."

"Anyway, you hit that damn piana the way you do, played it just like you play it now, and he stopped—I mean, *stopped*— put that tape in that machine and started the motor up. Played for somethin' like three hours and a half, didn't ya? Somethin' like that. Then I ask him, I say, 'Well, what d'ya think 'bout it?' He says, 'I wouldn't had that tape goin' I didn't think it was all right.' "

"That sonofabitch."

Jack Clement remembered that day, too. "At that time," he said, "there were a lot of people comin' to Sun Records to get auditions and that. This was after Elvis and some other things had happened. I listened to a lot of 'em, but I didn't listen to all of 'em.

"I remember when Jerry Lee came in, I was back in the studio, back in the control room. The receptionist came back and said, 'There's this kid here who says he plays piano like Chet Atkins plays guitar.' This made no sense at all, so I said, 'Oh, yeah? Bring him on back.' So Jerry Lee came back with his daddy. He was confident, but he wasn't real pushy or anything. You could tell he was a little *overt*. But I was kind of used to that; it was part of the rock-'n'-roll thing. I wasn't shying away from overtness.

"We sat down at the little spinet piano, and, sure enough, he played somethin' that sounded like Chet Atkins. 'So what else do you do?' I said. 'Well, I sing.' So I got him to sing, but it was all country stuff. I did run a little tape, just him and the piano, singin' 'Seasons of My Heart' and two or three other country-type things. He didn't sing any rock 'n' roll for me. I told him that the bottom had sort of dropped out of the country business. The only people that were actually sellin' big in country at that time, I think, were George Jones, a few others.

And, of course, Sun Records wasn't country-oriented at that point. So I told him if he could come up with some rock 'n' roll we could probably do somethin'. I told him to go write some rock 'n' roll."

After they left the Sun studio that afternoon, Jerry Lee and Elmo went to Meteor Records on Chelsea Avenue, in the black part of town. They met with Lester Bihari, the man who had founded Meteor in late 1952. Like Sun, Meteor had begun as a blues label, but since that magic summer of 1954 Bihari had been putting out some whitefolk rock 'n' roll, records by men such as Bud Deckelmen, Malcolm Yelvington, Junior Thompson, Charlie Feathers, and Bill Bowen. None of these rockabilly records sold very well (in fact, Meteor's only hit had been its first release, "I Believe" by the legendary black guitarist Elmore James), and by this November day in 1956 Meteor was on unsolid ground. Lester Bihari was enthusiastic about Jerry Lee, but Jerry Lee and Elmo were not enthusiastic about him. "Boy, I'm glad I didn't get tied up with that guy," Jerry Lee would later say. "He was jumpin' around, carryin' on like he was in-sane. Nice ol' cat, but I'm glad I didn't get tied up with 'im."

It was at the old Black River house, where Jerry Lee had left the Starck upright when moving to the downtown apartment with Jane, that he wrote his song. Frankie Jean and Linda Gail were there. Jane was there, and little Jerry Lee, Jr., and that other child who would not, even unto his tenth generation, enter into the kingdom of God. Jerry Lee sat there at the piano, laboring.

He had the music—a fast, driving, cut-time boogie—but the words were coming slowly. He was trying to write a song about dark solitude and long, nighttime journeying, and about what lay at the close of that journeying. This last part was what troubled him. He sat there playing that fast, hard boogie, trying to figure out what it truly was that lay at the end of all night. He looked around him at the weaker vessels, sisters and wife, and at the blooded issue, true son and spurious, of that wife, and it came to him: "There'll be a weddin' at the end of the road." But Frankie Jean and Jane ridiculed his refrain.

"We were laughin'," Frankie Jean recalled, "sayin', 'That doesn't sound right.' Because the road in the song just went to a dead end. And so we's tryin' to get him to put, 'I'll be waitin' at the end of the road.' And eventually he did, sure did— changed it from 'wedding' to 'waiting.' We kept tellin' him, 'That's not your style, that weddin' business.' He'll never give us credit for it, but it's true."

> Well, the way is dark,
> Night is long,
> I don't care if I never get home!
> I'm waitin' at the end of the
>   road!

He had his song, and he sang it in the late afternoon, imagining himself to be singing it for Sam Phillips. After he sang it, he beheld himself in a mirror, looking sideways. He saw waves of hair the color of burnt gold, eyes that were like those of a suddenly snared but uncrying hawk. He narrowed them, still looking sideways. He was twenty-one, too old to be controlled. He saw that. He saw Mamie's darling boy, and he saw the Killer.

Jerry Lee wanted to return to Memphis, but he hesitated. Then his cousin JW Brown came to Ferriday, looking for him. Like his brother Otis, the fiddler whom Jerry Lee had met a few years before at the Little Club in Monroe, JW hankered to make music. On leave from his job at the electric company in

JW Brown, 1958.

Memphis following an injury, JW had now come to Jerry Lee with the hope that they might put together a band.

These cousins had never met. JW (his parents had given him no Christian name, only these two lone letters) was one of the four children born to Elmo's sister Jane and her husband, Henry. He was ten years older than Jerry Lee, and he lived in suburban Memphis with his wife, Clara Lois, and their two children, Rusty, who was not quite two, and Myra Gale, who had turned twelve the previous July.

When Jerry Lee told JW that he had been to Sun Records, JW urged him to return. They drove to Memphis together, to JW's house at 4908 East Shore Drive, out near Coro Lake. Jerry Lee was introduced to JW's wife, then to his little blue-eyed, brown-haired daughter.

Jerry Lee looked at Myra Gale, his twelve-year-old cousin. She was prettier than Pandora. He felt something that he had not felt before—something that he had not even known to exist. Myra Gale felt it, too. They did not say anything about it that night, nor for many nights after that. But they both knew that if ever on God's green earth there had been love at first sight, this was it.

Ten

Jack Clement had been listening to the tape of Jerry Lee's audition, and he had played it for Sam Phillips. "I really liked it," Jack said. "I was personally into country, even though Sun Records didn't seem to be at that time. I got to listenin' to it, and I played it for different people. Sam heard it and liked it. On the tape box I had written a phone number where I could reach Jerry Lee, and I was right on the verge of callin' him about three weeks later, 'cause Sam had heard it and really liked it. He thought we oughta try to do somethin' with the guy, even though it wasn't rock 'n' roll. He really liked his singin' and his piano style."

When Jerry Lee returned to Sun with JW Brown, Sam Phillips was again out of town, vacationing in Miami. "That was the first time I met JW," Jack Clement said. "He was gonna be Jerry Lee's manager, or somethin' like that. Since his first visit, Jerry Lee had grown some fuzz on his chin, tryin' to cultivate a goatee. It looked rather unsightly, and I suggested that he might wanna get rid of it."

This was on Monday. Clement told Jerry Lee to come back to the studio on Thursday. Then he called three Sun session men—drummer James Van Eaton and guitarists Roland Janes and Billy Lee Riley—and he told them to come in on Thursday, too.

Jerry Lee spent the next three nights at JW's house. Myra Gale cooked a pizza for him on Wednesday night, and as he ate it he watched her smile. The next morning, Jerry Lee and JW drove into town early. Jack Clement saw that Jerry Lee still had his goatee and that JW was carrying a guitar. Clement told JW that he ought to learn to play the electric bass, instead of the guitar, if he wanted to play with Jerry Lee, and eventually that is what JW did.

"I walked into the studio," remembers James Van Eaton, the drummer, who was eighteen at the time, "and there was Jerry Lee and JW Brown. JW had him this big blond Silvertone gittar that he'd bought over at Sears, y'know. Jerry had him a goatee. They were a really weird-lookin' pair."

"The first song we cut," said Jack Clement, "was that rockin' thing that he'd written, 'End of the Road.' Then we did that old Gene Autry song, 'You're the Only Star (In My Blue Heaven),' which had always been a waltz, but Jerry Lee turned it into a boogie-woogie sorta thing. That was my favorite one that he'd come up with."

Toward the end of the session, Clement asked Jerry Lee if he knew "Crazy Arms," the country hit by Ray Price that had been on the charts since the past spring. Jerry Lee had performed the song with Johnny Littlejohn's band, and he told Clement that "I know some of it."

"So we cut it," Clement said. "We cut it with only the spinet piano and the drums. I put thumbtacks in the piano, then miked it down below, stuck the mike down by the feet there. It gave it a kind of different sound, almost like a big piano. Eventually, Sam broke down and bought us a better piano, a little Steinway baby grand.

"Anyway, while we were cuttin' this thing, Billy Lee Riley was in the crapper. At the very end of the song, Riley strolls back in, and he thought we were just messin' around—which we were. Turned out to be a record, however. He picks up his electric guitar and hits some bad ol' chord right as Jerry Lee was finishin'. We just left it on. Strangest endin' on record."

After the session, Jack told Jerry Lee to hang around town until Sam returned. He took him to the Cotton Club, across the Mississippi River in West Memphis, Arkansas, and he got him some work with Clyde Leoppard and the Snearly Ranch Boys, a local country dance band that played frequently with Sun artists.

When Sam Phillips arrived in town on Saturday, Jack Clement took him into the control room. They sat there at the small, 7½-ips, two-track console, and Jack punched up Jerry Lee's version of "Crazy Arms."

Sam Phillips, who in his thirty-three years had heard more fine and singular music than most men hear in a lifetime, closed his eyes and listened to the raunchy little piano introduction with which Jerry Lee had begun the song. The introduction lasted barely ten seconds. At the end of those seconds, Sam Phillips abruptly opened his eyes, reached out, and stopped the tape.

"I can sell that," he said.

BEHOLD
A SHAKING

One

Within an hour, Sam made an acetate dub of Jerry Lee's "Crazy Arms," and he took it that night to Dewey Phillips, the WHBQ disc jockey who had premiered Elvis's first record back in July, 1954. When Dewey played Jerry Lee's recording on the air, the response was immense and excited, as it had been for Elvis's record. By the following Tuesday, Sam had copies of the record pressed and shipped. This was the fastest—barely five days from taping to distribution—that any Sun record had ever been released.

Jerry Lee held the record in his hands and he stared at its brown-and-yellow label:

END OF THE ROAD
(Jerry Lewis)
JERRY LEE LEWIS
With His
Pumping Piano

He stared at it, not only with his own eyes, but with the eyes of Old Man Lewis, and of Mamie and of Elmo, and of Lee Calhoun and of Johnny Littlejohn, and of Miss Nellie Jackson, and of the Holy Ghost. And he grinned like a fool, for in all those eyes he was redeemed.

The record did not make the charts, national or local, but it sold well in the South and received attention from the trade weekly *Billboard* in its country reviews section of December 22. "An exceptionally strong entrant in this flavor-packed disk. His reading of 'Crazy Arms' shows a powerful feeling for country blues, and his sock warbling is accompanied by a Domino-type piano backing which brings a distinct New Orleans feeling to the rendition. Flip ['End of the Road'] is another honey, right in the rhythm groove and abetted by the same piano beat. Distinctly smart wax."

Jack Clement had asked Jerry Lee to come to the studio on the afternoon of December 4 to play piano at a Carl Perkins session. A little less than a year before, Perkins had recorded "Blue Suede Shoes," and it had become one of the biggest hits of 1956, crossing over from country to pop to R & B. It was the best-selling record in Sun's brief history, and both Sam and Carl were eager to have its success repeated. Of the five songs recorded on December 4, Sam chose to release "Your True Love," which Perkins had recently written, and "Matchbox," a hard-rocking version of a blues song that had first been cut, as "Matchbox Blues," by Blind Lemon Jefferson in 1927. Neither of these recordings achieved the success that Sam and Carl hoped they would, and Carl Perkins, who had given rock 'n' roll one of its few true anthems, slowly fell to that place where fame repeats its own name, endlessly slurring through thick, whorish lips.

Jerry Lee was to be paid fifteen dollars for his work that

afternoon, and that sounded fine to him. He enjoyed playing with Perkins, whose records he liked, and he enjoyed meeting Johnny Cash, another Sun star, who came to the session at Carl's invitation. But most of all he enjoyed—rather, savored—meeting the one person whom no one had expected to be there, the one person who had been on his mind more than any other man in recent days. Yes, he savored meeting him, he truly did.

Since leaving Sun the previous year, Elvis had visited at the old studio every once in a while. "He'd just drop by, usually in the afternoon," Jack Clement said. "He'd pop in on his motor- cycle, hang around with us for a spell. One time he came in, we were shootin' craps in the control room. He had on a damn motorcycle suit; he looked like a cop. We thought we'd been busted."

Elvis arrived at the Sun studio this December 4 afternoon with Marilyn Evans, a pretty nineteen-year-old chorus girl he had brought home from the New Frontier in Las Vegas. Every- one in the studio gathered around Elvis—him, the most fam- ous person in the world. Elvis sat at the piano and began to move his fingers across the keys tentatively. Carl Perkins's lit- tle band (his brothers J.B. and Clayton on rhythm guitar and bass; W. S. "Fluke" Holland on drums) picked up their in- struments and followed Elvis's unsure sounds. Soon Elvis, Carl, Cash, and Jerry Lee were singing together. Jack Clement turned on the tape recorder and Sam Phillips telephoned the Memphis *Press-Scimitar*. Within a few minutes, columnist Robert Johnson ("TV News and Views") and staff photogra- pher George Pierce arrived at the studio. By then the band had quit, but Elvis, Carl, Cash, and Jerry Lee were still singing at the piano. After the photographer took pictures, Johnny Cash, who had been singing bass, left to go shopping with his wife,

Vivian. The three remaining men continued to sing. Perkins, who was a strong singer on his own, sang softly, almost shyly, in the presence of Elvis. But Jerry Lee sang like a hawk.

They sang "Blueberry Hill," then they started in on gospel: "Just a Little Talk with Jesus," "Lonesome Valley," "I Shall Not Be Moved" (after which Jerry Lee proclaimed, "Boy, this is fun. I like that"), "Peace in the Valley," and "Down by the Riverside." After Elvis performed a brief, sarcastic imitation of Hank Snow, they returned to gospel: "Farther Along," "Blessed Jesus, Hold My Hand," "Jericho Road," and "I Just Can't Make It by Myself." Then came a medley of Bill Monroe songs from the late forties—"Little Cabin on the Hill," "The Summer's Come and Gone," "I Hear a Sweet Voice Calling," "Sweetheart, You Done Me Wrong"—followed by a version of Wynn Stewart's recent "Keeper of the Keys" and a few bars of Pat Boone's new record, "Don't Forbid Me," at the end of which Elvis commented that the song had been written for him, that it "stayed over my house for ages, man. I never did see it. Y'know, so much junk layin' around and all."

Elvis had heard Jerry Lee's record, and when Jerry Lee sang a piece of "Crazy Arms" Elvis smiled and said, "The wrong man's been settin' here at this piano."

"Well, I been wantin' to tell you that," Jerry Lee said, smiling, too, and looking into Elvis's eyes, clutching them for a moment with his own, feeling what was in them, then discarding them. "Scoot over!"

In his newspaper column the next day Robert Johnson wrote of the chilly afternoon past:

I never had a better time than yesterday when I dropped in at Sam Phillips' Sun Record bedlam on Union and Marshall. It was what you might call a barrel-house of fun. Carl Perkins was in a recording session, and he has one that's going to hit as hard as "Blue Suede Shoes." We're trying to arrange an advance audition for you Memphis fans before the song is released in January. Johnny Cash dropped in. Jerry Lee Lewis was there, too, and then Elvis stopped by.

Elvis headed for the piano and started to Fats Domino it on "Blueberry Hill." The joint was really rocking before they got thru.

Elvis is high on Jerry Lee Lewis. "That boy can go," he said. "I think he has a great future ahead of him. He has a different style, and the way he plays piano just gets inside me."

I never saw Elvis more likeable than he was just fooling around with these other fellows who have the same interests he does.

If Sam Phillips had been on his toes, he'd have turned the recorder on when that very unrehearsed but talented bunch got to cutting up on "Blueberry Hill" and a lot of other songs. That quartet could sell a million.

A few days later, Sam Phillips sent a press release to the disc jockeys on the Sun mailing list. The seven-by-twelve-inch sheet reproduced Robert Johnson's column, along with George Pierce's photograph of the Million Dollar Quartet. The bottom of the sheet carried a message in Sam's handwriting:

Our Only Regret!
That each and everyone of you wonderful D.J.'s who are responsible for these boys being among the best known and liked in show business could not be there *too*!

We thought however that you might like to read first hand about our little shindig—it was a *dilly*!

Sincerely grateful,
Sam Phillips

Jerry Lee returned to Ferriday for Christmas, bringing with him the testaments of his victorious journey upriver: copies of Sam's press release, copies of his record, 45s and big, heavy 78s. His kin beheld these things in pride or in envy, each according to the bent of his soul, and they listened, likewise, as he spoke of royalties and advances and percentages of the gate. When he had done with his speaking, he patted Uncle Lee on the back, for now, more than ever before, they were kindred.

After Christmas Jerry Lee cleared out the garage apartment on Louisiana Avenue. He drove to Memphis with Jane and Junior (the other, disowned child, Ronnie Guy, had been given to Jane's sister) and moved into a little red house he had rented not far from the Sun studio.

In January, 1957, Jerry Lee worked as a session pianist for Sun singers Warren Smith and Billy Lee Riley. The first record he cut with Riley, a twenty-three-year-old rocker from Pocahontas, Arkansas, was "Flyin' Saucers Rock 'n' Roll." The record became a local sensation, and Riley renamed his band the Little Green Men. When the band went out on the road, Jerry Lee joined them.

"He played piano with us and sang on a few numbers," said James Van Eaton, the drummer in Riley's band. "He was just like all the rest of us back then. He was broke, needed the money, so he played with us a couple of times. We played in Arkansas, Mississippi, places like that, local clubs around here. Bob Neal used to book all that stuff, and sometimes it seemed that just about the only places he knew to book anybody was Arkansas and Mississippi, Tennessee. Y'know, National Guard Armories, that kinda business."

On January 30 Jerry Lee played at the Billy Lee Riley session that resulted in Riley's most successful record, "Red Hot." The record opened with Riley growling, "My gal is red hot!" To which Jerry Lee and the rest of the band yelled in loud response, "Your gal ain't doodily-squat!"

This was the last time that Jerry Lee consented to work as a session musician. Though his own record was not a hit, he told Sam Phillips that he would no longer perform behind any other man—that from here on in Jerry Lee Lewis would work only for Jerry Lee Lewis.

"Sam would ask him to play piano on a session, and it got to where he just didn't wanna do it," James Van Eaton said. "He started realizin', I guess, that these people would never help him, so, what the heck, he wouldn't play for them, either."

Bob Neal, the taciturn thirty-nine-year-old Memphis booking agent who had been Elvis's first manager, and who now booked most of the Sun acts through his new Stars Incorporated agency, began to book Jerry Lee as a separate act. Jerry Lee continued to work with Billy Lee Riley's band, using it as his own on those nights when Riley did not.

Jerry Lee's first important booking was on February 23, as a guest on "The Big D Jamboree," the country-and-Western show that was broadcast every Saturday night from Ed McLemore's Sportatorium on lower Industrial Boulevard in Dallas, not far from Jerry Lee's alma mater, Southwestern Bible Institute. He was so well received by the Dallas crowd that he was invited to return the following month.

On the night before his debut on "The Big D Jamboree," Jerry Lee had played at a small club in Blytheville, Arkansas, about sixty miles north of Memphis. It was at this club that

Jerry Lee performed "Whole Lotta Shakin' Goin' On" for the
first time since leaving Johnny Littlejohn's band. Remembering only some of the lyrics, he spewed forth new words.

> *Come on over, baby, whole lotta shakin' goin' on;*
> *Yes, I said, come on over baby; baby, you can't go wrong;*
> *We ain't fakin', whole lotta shakin' goin' on.*
> *Well, I said, come on over, baby, we got kickin' in the barn-*
> *uh!*
> *Oo—huh?—come on over, baby; baby, got the bull by the horn-*
> *uh!*
>
> *We ain't fakin', whole lotta shakin' goin' on.*
> *Well, I said, shake, baby, shake;*
> *I said, shake, baby, shake;*
> *I said, shake it, baby, shake it;*
> *Let it shake, make it shake.*
> *Come on over, whole lotta shakin' goin' on!*
> *Aw, let's go!*

And he shut his mouth and pounded the piano, and as he
pounded it he saw that women were pressed against the stage,
their ripe, cinctured breasts heaving synchronously with his
pounding. He saw that their mouths were more open than
closed, and that stray curls were stuck to their foreheads with
dripping sweat; and he saw jealousy in the young redneck faces
of the Arkansas boys. He pounded faster and harder, his fingers talons of ravishing puissance, and he felt the rush of neon
gas shoot from his lungs as he saw those girls, quivering and
wet, following him to hell with their painted mouths open.

> *Well, I said, come on over, baby, we got kickin' in the*
> *barn.*

Whose barn? What barn? My barn!
Come on over, baby; baby, got the bull by the horn.
We ain't fakin', whole lotta shakin' goin' on!

Some of the redneck boys had now withdrawn and clustered
at the bar, drinking in violent cowardice among themselves.
The girls' heads were moving up and down furiously. They
were possessed. Jerry Lee lowered his voice, alternating song
with speech, addressing the girls, commanding them.

Easy now—shake it!
Aw, shake it, baby—yeah!
You can shake it one time for me—aww.
Uh-wuh-hey-ell, I said, come on over, baby, whole lotta
  shakin' goin' on
Now let's git real low one time—shake, baby, shake.
All ya gotta do, honey, is stand that thing in one little
  ol' spot;
Wiggle it aroun' just a little bit.
And that's when ya got somethin'—yeah.
Oh, baby, whole lotta shakin' goin' on.

He paused, let his eyes sweep across the eyes of the girls. He
could smell the serpent that slithered among their narrow an-
kles, and he could smell the odor of their oblation. He howled.

Now let's go one time!
Shake it, baby, shake it!
Shake it, make it shake!
Oo, shake, baby!—come on, babe;
Shake, baby, shake!
Come on over! Whole lotta shakin' goin'
  on!

He left the stage as a godlike man, and he drank from the weaker vessel and cast it to the ground, then went south to Dallas.

A few days after he returned from Texas, he went into the studio with drummer James Van Eaton and guitarist Roland Janes to record a song that Jack Clement had written called "It'll Be Me." This was an upbeat dance tune about metamorphosis that had come to Clement while shitting. "If you find a turd in your toilet bowl, it'll be me, and I'll be lookin' for you," was how the song began. Now, in the studio, Clement changed "turd in your toilet bowl" to "lump in your sugar bowl."

"We were cuttin' the song, workin' pretty hard at it for a while, and I felt like we oughta get off of it, try somethin' else for a spell," Jack remembered. "I left the control room, walked into the studio. Van Eaton, one of 'em, piped up and said, 'Hey, Jerry, why don't you do that thing you did the other night?' So all I did was walk back into the control room and turn on the machine. We didn't run it down or nothin'. The mike balance, our four or five mikes, was the same. I just simply turned on the machine, mixed it on the fly. We didn't even play it back at that point. We played it back later. Once we got to playin' it back, we played it again and again. Loved it."

Jerry Lee returned to "The Big D Jamboree" on March 30, this time sharing the guest spot with the Five Strings, a rockabilly band from Denton, Texas. For the next five nights he traveled with Johnny Cash and Onie Wheeler, playing in Little Rock, Monroe, Sheffield, Jackson, Memphis, and Odessa.

On April 15 Sam released Jerry Lee's record of "Whole Lotta Shakin' Goin' On." A week later, on April 21, Jerry Lee, along with Johnny Cash, Carl Perkins, and Wanda Jackson, commenced a long tour of Canada booked by Bob Neal. Jerry

Lee was no longer using Billy Lee Riley's band, but instead the three-piece group that had been backing singer Warren Smith: drummer Jimmy Lott, guitarist Al Hopson, and bass player Marcus Van Story.

Starting in Sault Sainte Marie, Ontario, the show worked its way west across Canada at a devastating pace—from Ontario to Manitoba, to Saskatchewan and Alberta, to British Columbia, then back to Alberta and Saskatchewan, often traveling more than five hundred miles from one night's show to the next. It was during this long tour that Jerry Lee discovered that Johnny Cash was addicted to pills and that Carl Perkins was an alcoholic.

The convoy emerged from Canada on May 12 and performed that night in Billings, Montana. By then Jerry Lee had honed his stage act to a thing of great majesty and had taken to closing every performance with "Whole Lotta Shakin' Goin' On."

"He'd jump up and kick the piano stool back with his foot," remembered Marcus Van Story, who played an Epiphone bull fiddle behind Jerry Lee. "He'd play the piano with his feet—that kinda stuff. He was a good one on stage, yessir. They loved him."

Without a break, the touring Sun acts joined forces with the Sonny James Show on May 13, playing one-nighters straight through to the twenty-fifth, when Jerry Lee made his third appearance on "The Big D Jamboree."

After more than a month on the road, Jerry Lee returned to Memphis, exhausted and broke. "I was gettin' a hundred dollars a day," he later said of that long spring tour of 1957. "I left home with fifty dollars in my pocket, an' when I came back I had about twenty-five. Don't know how it happened, but it did."

Traveling through the South that May, Jerry Lee was aware that his record was getting a lot of airplay, and that his name was no longer wholly unknown. "A lot of people," Marcus Van Story said, "would come up to us before the shows an' ask, 'Who's that black guy on piano who's got that record out?' They thought Jerry Lee was a black guy. We used to kid him 'bout that."

"Whole Lotta Shakin' Goin' On" entered the Memphis C & W charts, in the number two rank, during the third week of May, a month after it had been released. The May 27 issue of *Billboard,* in its pop section, said that "Lewis comes through with what should be a sure hit, in a driving blues shouter in the typical Sun tradition. Flip rockabilly ['It'll Be Me'] could go, too, on strength of another top performance and cute tune." The same issue of *Billboard* also praised the record in its R & B section, which was usually devoted purely to black acts. The next week, *Billboard* showed that the record had hit the number one position on the Memphis C & W charts, and, in "This Week's C&W Best Buys," remarked that "This platter by Lewis is taking off like wildfire. Tho in release only a short while, all areas list it as a top seller. It should also do well in pop and r.&b. markets."

On June 12 the record entered the national C & W charts, and a week later it broke into the pop charts. Life would never be the same for Mamie's darling boy, nor for the Killer.

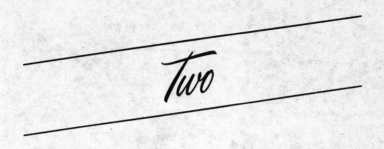

Two

Fame lifted her skirt for the final wild son. As the summer
passed, hot Southern day upon hot Southern night, the sound
of "Whole Lotta Shakin' Goin' On" grew louder and more
ominous. It was everywhere, blasting forth like thunder without rain from cars and bars and all the open windows of the
unsaved. Its wicked rhythm devoured the young of the land. It
bloodied virgins and stirred new housewives to recall things
they never spoke of. It inspired boys to reinvent themselves as
flaming new creatures and to seek detumescence without ruth.

By the end of July, "Whole Lotta Shakin' Goin' On" had
sold about 100,000 copies. Then it ran into trouble. Many
people feared the song and its singer. Even some who liked
Elvis damned Jerry Lee as lascivious and evil. Mothers smelled
his awful presence in the laundry of their daughters, and
preachers stood before their flocks and railed against him and

At the Sun piano the summer that fame lifted her skirt.

his sinful song. Slowly, radio stations began to ban the record, and it was heard less and less.

Judd Phillips, Sam's brother and Sun's promotion man, took Jerry Lee to New York and presented him to Henry Frankel, the talent coordinator for NBC, and Jules Green, who managed Steve Allen. They arranged for Jerry Lee to audition for Allen, and Allen immediately invited Jerry Lee to appear on his TV program. Then Judd had Sun ship large orders of "Whole Lotta Shakin' Goin' On" to every retail outlet in the country. This was a great gamble, for if Jerry Lee's performance on "The Steve Allen Show" was not a success, those truckloads of records would be returned to Sun, and Sam would have to absorb the loss, or perhaps even fall.

"The Steve Allen Show" of July 28 opened with a skit by Shelley Winters and Anthony Franciosa, in which Franciosa reenacted his marriage proposal to Winters. (The actors had been married three months to the day.) Jerry Lee waited backstage, hearing the audience laugh, and he may have been wondering what the audience's reaction would be if he and Jane and Jane's brothers were out there reenacting instead. Then the Four Coins were on stage, and Jerry Lee listened, and he knew that those boys had grown up very far from Haney's Big House. Then out came a Miss United States who had been disqualified when it was revealed that she was a Mrs. Finally, with less than five minutes left to the show, Jerry Lee was given his signal. He sat at the big piano and he looked sideways at the camera, eyeballed it the way he had looked at those girls in that Arkansas beer joint, and then he began to play the piano and howl about the shaking that was going on. He rose, still pounding, and he kicked the piano stool back. It shot across the stage, tumbling, skidding, almost hitting one of those Coin boys. Steve Allen laughed and threw the stool back, then threw other furniture, and Jerry Lee played some high notes with the heel of his shoe. Then he stopped and looked at the camera sideways again. Neither he nor Steve Allen had ever heard louder applause.

The very next day, Jerry Lee's record began to rise anew, and nothing—not preachers, not mothers—could contain it. Judd and Jerry Lee stayed in New York for a while. On August 2, the Friday night after his debut on "The Steve Allen Show," Jerry Lee performed on Alan Freed's ABC-TV show, "The Big Beat." Nine days later, on August 11, he returned to "The Steve Allen Show," and once again he closed the show and drove the people wild.

"Whole Lotta Shakin' Goin' On" rose higher and higher on both the pop and country charts. During the last week of August, it hit the R & B charts as well. At the end of the month, Jerry Lee's record held the number one positions on the C & W and R & B charts—only Elvis before him had placed a single record at the top of both these charts—then it rose to the top of the pop charts. By summer's end, the record had sold well over a million copies.

Jerry Lee drove to Ferriday in a Cadillac, triumphantly. He embraced his mother and father, and Linda Gail, who was now ten and very tall, and Frankie Jean, who was almost thirteen and married to a local boy named New. He embraced Aunt Stella and Uncle Lee; and Uncle Lee, who was in his sixties now but still riding a horse daily across his many miles of black earth, smiled at Jerry Lee and told him that he had done good.

Jerry Lee rented a fine new home for his parents, a little green house near the Church of God, where he had preached, on Mississippi Avenue—a home with running water and bathtub and commode. Then he purchased them an even finer, bigger home in the Ridgecrest subdivision south of town. He told his daddy that the days of farming were done and that all days hence would be of harvest. But Elmo grew restless of this new life without the balm of toil, and Jerry Lee bought him a farm in Clayton, then a second farm in Dunbarton, a beautiful place near the clear-running Tensas. He bought him cattle and hogs, a tractor, and a combine; and Elmo traveled among his farms and homes in a new black Cadillac, working and grinning and drinking and telling tales.

The wealth seemed to be endless and fortune a faithful bride at Jerry Lee's feet. With his cousin JW Brown on Fender bass and Russell Smith on drums, Jerry Lee roamed the country, making the Devil's music for a thousand dollars a night, and receiving thousands more every week in record-sales royalties. But the Devil derided his money and would not let loose his lungs.

During the third week of August, Jerry Lee recorded "Great Balls of Fire," a song written by Jack Hammer, a New York session pianist, and Otis Blackwell, the eccentric black songwriter and singer who had supplied Elvis with his two biggest hits, "Don't Be Cruel" and "All Shook Up." Blackwell brought "Great Balls of Fire" to Jerry Lee after seeing him on "The Steve Allen Show."

Sam Phillips and Jack Clement spent several days in the studio with Jerry Lee working on "Great Balls of Fire." At one of these sessions, everyone in the studio—Jerry Lee, Sam Phillips, Jack Clement, drummer James Van Eaton, bass player Billy Lee Riley—got to drinking. Jerry Lee became filled with the Holy Ghost, and he decided that the song "Great Balls of Fire" was of the devil and that to sing it was to sin. Sam Phillips argued against Jerry Lee's stand. Jack Clement switched on the tape and recorded the argument.

"H-E-L-L!" Jerry Lee loudly spelled.

"I don't believe this," Sam Phillips muttered.

"Great Godamighty, great balls of fire!" James Van Eaton proclaimed mockingly.

"That's right!" hollered Billy Lee Riley, right behind him.

"I don't believe it," Sam repeated.

"It says make merry with the joy of God *only*," Jerry Lee yelled. "But when it comes to *worldly* music, rock 'n' roll . . ."

"Pluck it out!" Billy Lee Riley shouted.

". . . anything like that," Jerry Lee went on, fast, driven. "You have done brought yourself into the world, and you're in the world, and you're still a sinner. You're a sinner and unless you be saved and borned again and be made as a little chile and walk before God and be holy—and, brother, I mean you got to be *so* pure. No sin shall enter there—*no sin*! For it says *no sin*. It don't say just a little bit; it says *no sin shall enter there*. Brother, not one little bit. You got to *walk* and *talk* with God to go to heaven. You got to be *so* good."

"Hallelujah," Riley said.

"All right," Sam said. "Now look, Jerry, religious conviction doesn't mean anything resembling extremism. All right. Do you mean to tell me that you're gonna take the Bible, that you're gonna take God's word, and that you're gonna revolutionize the whole universe? Now, listen. Jesus Christ was sent here by God Almighty—"

"Right!" said Jerry Lee.

"Did He convince, did He save all of the people in the world?"

"Naw, but He tried to!"

"He sure did. Now, wait a minute. Jesus Christ came into this world. He tolerated man. He didn't preach from one pulpit. He went around and did good."

"That's right! He preached everywhere!"

"Everywhere."

"He preached on land!"

"Everywhere. That's right, that's right."

"He preached on the water!"

"That's right, that's exactly right. Now—"

"Man, He done everything! He *healed*!"

"Now, now, here, here's the difference—"

"Are you followin' those that heal? Like Jesus Christ did? Well, it's happenin' every day!"

"What d'ya mean . . . you . . . what . . . I, I . . . what—"

"The *blind* had eyes opened. The *lame* were made to walk."

"Jerry, Jesus Christ—"

"The crippled were made to walk."

"Jesus Christ, in my opinion, is just as real today as He was when He came into this world."

"Right! Right! You're so right you don't know what you're sayin'!"

"Now, I will say, more so—"

"Aw, let's cut it," Riley interrupted disgustedly.

"It'll never sell, man," Van Eaton said to him. "It's not commercial."

"Wait, wait, wait just a minute," Sam said, throwing his arms up, "we can't, we got to—now, look, listen, I'm tellin' you outa my heart, and I have studied the Bible a little bit—"

"Well, I have too," said Jerry Lee. "I studied it through and through and through and through, and I know what I'm talkin' about."

"Jerry. Jerry. If you think that you can't, can't do good if you're a rock-'n'-roll exponent—"

"You can do good, Mr. Phillips, don't get me wrong—"

"Now, wait, wait, listen. When I say *do good*—"

"You can have a kind heart!"

"I don't mean, I don't mean just—"

"You can help people!"

"You can save souls!"

"*No! No! No! No!*"

"*Yes!*"

"*How can the Devil save souls? What are you talkin' about?*"

"Listen, listen . . ."

"Man, I got *the Devil* in me! If I didn't have, I'd be a Christian!"

"Well, you may have him—"

"*Jesus!*" Jerry Lee yelled, pressing his fists to his breast. "Heal this man! He cast the devil out. The devil says, Where can I go? He says, Can I go into this *swine?* He says, Yeah, go into him. Didn't he go into him?"

"Jerry, the point I'm tryin' to make is, if you believe in what you're singin', you got no alternative whatsoever, out of—listen!— out of—"

"Mr. Phillips! I don't care. It ain't what you believe, *it's what's written in the Bible!*"

"Well, wait a minute."

"It's what's *there*, Mr. Phillips."

"No, no."

"It ain't what you believe, it's just what's there."

"No, by gosh, if it's not what you believe, then how do you *interpret* the Bible?"

"Man alive," moaned Riley.

"Huh? How do you interpret the Bible if it's not what you believe?" repeated Sam.

"Well, it's just not what you believe, you just can't—"

"*Let's cut it, man!*" Riley screamed.

"No, you got to—" began Sam.

"You can talk . . ." Jerry Lee turned away from him, as from a fool.

"No, here's the thing—"

"You can talk, and you can talk . . ."

Between midnight and dawn they finally cut it, in violence, anger, and weariness. It had been difficult, but in the end Sam Phillips knew that he had a hit, a record of unrelenting rhythm and mindless venereal splendor. Jack Clement made a comment about splitting the royalties with the Holy Ghost, but no one laughed.

On August 22 a United Press story suggested that Jerry Lee was fast surpassing Elvis as the boy king of rock 'n' roll. The story stated that "Whole Lotta Shakin' Goin' On" was selling at a rate of more than 10,000 copies a day. Judd Phillips was quoted as saying that Jerry Lee didn't shake like Elvis, that he "Doesn't have to. When he feels like it, he just jumps up and kicks the piano stool across the stage and plays standing up. And his legs get real stiff. What's different about him is that he's got a beat, a rhythm, like you've never felt." Referring to Elvis's sale to RCA Victor, Judd said that his brother and he "don't aim to sell any more artists to anybody—particularly not Lewis."

The following week, Jerry Lee signed a contract to perform in *Jamboree,* a low-budget Warner Bros. film being directed by Roy Lockwood, with Otis Blackwell serving as musical director. Barely held together by a story line concerning the woes of two love-struck young singers, played by Paul Carr and Freda Holloway, *Jamboree* was to include no fewer than twenty-one songs in eighty-six minutes of film. Jerry Lee and Fats Domino were to share the top billing (the only actor of any stature in the film was Robert Pastene, who had played Buck Rogers on television), followed by Buddy Knox, Jimmy Bowen, Charlie Gracie, the Four Coins, Carl Perkins, Slim Whitman, Connie Francis, Frankie Avalon, and others. Each of these acts was to be introduced by a different disc jockey—in Jerry Lee's case,

Ray Perkins of KIMN in Denver. Jerry Lee went to New York to lip-synch "Great Balls of Fire" before the movie cameras. He did not want to lip-synch; it seemed unnatural.

"Gene Autry never did it like this," he said. But a man in sunglasses, a man whose hands trembled, told him that Gene Autry would never have it any other way.

Three

His marriage to Jane was irreparable. Execration and fury, which had held them together like love, were now spent. Nothing remained, and they shared their little red house like narrow rays of cold winter light, intersecting occasionally, briefly, in harshness.

At the end of August, a secret informer told Jerry Lee that earlier in the summer, on July 17, while Jerry Lee had been playing in Youngstown, Ohio, Jane had lain beneath another man. Jerry Lee confronted Jane with this information. She took their child and left town, went to her older sister in Natchez.

On September 4 Jerry Lee filed a divorce petition in Circuit Court. The petition accused Jane of adultery, of frequenting bars, of cursing in public, and of using their home as a rendezvous for acts of immorality and wild drunken parties.

Jane Mitcham Lewis with Ronnie Guy and Jerry Lee, Jr. (Memphis, September, 1957).

Jane returned to Memphis with two Natchez attorneys, Carl Chadwick and William Riley. Retaining a third lawyer, Caruthers Ewing of Memphis, Jane filed in Circuit Court on September 20 an answer and cross-bill to Jerry Lee's petition for divorce. She denied that she had committed adultery and claimed to have spent the night in question at home with her child, her thirteen-year-old sister, who was married but separated from her husband, and her fifteen-year-old girl cousin. She also denied that she drank excessively or cursed in public. Asking that she be granted a divorce on grounds of cruel and inhuman treatment, abandonment, and nonsupport, her cross-bill accused Jerry Lee of deserting her twice, leaving her on one occasion with nothing but "eighty-two cents and six cans of milk to take care of self and child." The bill further claimed that Jerry Lee had a friend "who will go on the witness stand and testify that he is the father of the child [Ronnie Guy]," and that this was a part of Jerry Lee's "nefarious and illegal scheme to vilify this defendant and get out of his legal and moral obligation to support her and his children."

On the weekend after Jane filed her cross-bill, Jerry Lee appeared at the Apollo Theatre in Harlem for a brief set consisting of "Crazy Arms," "Mean Woman Blues," "Great Balls of Fire," and "Whole Lotta Shakin' Goin' On." This was the first time that he played for a predominantly black audience, and he was pleased, in an odd sort of way, to find that colored girls screamed for him almost as much as the white girls he had encountered in recent months. "There's a lot of animal vigor in the Jerry Lee Lewis Trio, an ofay rock 'n' roll team featuring the piano mitting and piping of Lewis," wrote a *Variety* reviewer who was at the Apollo that night. The reviewer went on to praise Jerry Lee's musical talent, but said that, "He would be wise to cut out some of his antics, for example, that of combing his hair after a frenetic number, and blowing his comb free in the direction of the audience. He could be the hillbilly he boasts that he is with good manners, too."

When he performed at Dement Field, a high-school football stadium in Galena Park, near Houston, Mickey Gilley came backstage to visit him after the show. The two cousins got to talking about old times in Ferriday, and about Jerry Lee's new-found wealth and fame.

"I got this new record comin' out that this little colored fella wrote for me," Jerry Lee said. "It's called 'Great Balls of Fire'."

Mickey thought that Jerry Lee was fooling with him. He did not believe that anyone would ever make a record with such a dirty title. But Jerry Lee sang some of the song for him, then looked sharply into Mickey's eyes. "It's gonna be a smash," he hissed, then entered a Cadillac and rode away, heading north toward Arkansas.

Mickey got to thinking, and it was not long before he went to Bill Quinn's Gold Star Studio in Houston, where he made his first record, "Tell Me Why" c/w "Oowee Baby." This record, released in 1958 on the Minor label, failed to bring either fame or fortune to Mickey; but he kept at it, making records for numerous local companies—Eric, Supreme, Lynn, Astro, and others—until, finally, he got what he sought.

Sun released "Great Balls of Fire" on November 3, when Jerry Lee appeared again on "The Steve Allen Show," this time in living color. *Billboard* reviewed the record enthusiastically in all three sections: pop, C & W, and R & B.

On November 15 Sam Phillips brought boxes of the record, along with copies of Jerry Lee's first EP, to the sixth annual D.J. Convention in Nashville. Phillips also took out a full-page advertisement for the record in *Billboard*—something that he had never done for any other Sun act.

On Thanksgiving Day, Jerry Lee performed the song on

Dick Clark's "American Bandstand," broadcast live from Philadelphia. (Also on the program that afternoon were Tom and Jerry, a young New York duo who would find fame eight years later as Simon and Garfunkel.) A week later, on December 6, he appeared on the CBS musical-variety series "The Howard Miller Show."

The movie *Jamboree,* which had been previewed in Hollywood on November 12, was now showing in neighborhood theaters throughout the country. (Newspapers reported that four ushers at the Center Theatre in Buffalo, New York, were stabbed during a gang fight that erupted while the image of Jerry Lee climaxed "Great Balls of Fire.")

By the second week of December "Great Balls of Fire" had broken into the Top Ten of the pop, C & W, and R & B charts, and had begun to ascend the British charts as well. It was the best-selling record in the history of Sun. Jerry Lee told his daddy that there were almost as many zeros on his checks as there had been *F*'s on his third-grade report card.

He had everything he wanted—everything but Myra Gale. Since his break-up with Jane in September, Jerry Lee had been living with the Brown family on East Shore Drive. Myra had dropped out of the eighth grade at Levi School not long after the start of the fall term, and what days Jerry Lee did not spend on the road he spent with Myra, under the unwary eyes of his cousin, Myra's father, JW, who continued to play bass in Jerry Lee's band. The sight and scent of her drove Jerry Lee wild, and his mind was like a tremulously held knife at the knot of her intact virginity. He was in love, lost in her.

On the morning of December 11, a cold and windy Wednesday, Jerry Lee and a lady friend drove south in his Cadillac to Fayette, Mississippi, the town where he and Jane had been married four years before. Between twelve and one in the afternoon, Jerry Lee and his lady friend entered the Jefferson

County Court House and applied for a marriage license. The lady friend stated that her name was Myra Gale Brown, and that her age was twenty. The license was issued, and Jerry Lee placed it in the glove compartment of his car, then drove back to Memphis with his lady friend, thanking her several times along the way.

The next day, Jerry Lee told JW and Lois that he was going to take Myra into town to see *Jamboree.* But instead of driving downtown, he turned south on Highway 55, toward the Mississippi line. Myra Gale looked at him, and she kept looking at him.

"Let's get married," he said.

"Let's go," she said.

They were married by Reverend M. C. Whitten in Hernando, the De Soto County seat, about fifteen miles south of Tennessee. They drove back toward Memphis through the long, late-afternoon shadows of winter. They stopped only once; then drove on, speaking very little.

They kept their marriage a secret for more than a week, living outwardly as cousins but inwardly as husband and wife. When Jerry Lee finally told JW and Lois that he had made their daughter his bride, they reacted in disbelief, then in anger. Lois bayed and besought the Lord's help, and JW threatened to skin Jerry Lee and annul the marriage in one fell swipe. But in time all violence ceased and a prosperous and precarious calm prevailed.

He had Myra now. He had everything. But still sanctuary escaped him. On a Sunday morning before Christmas, he got into his Cadillac and drove to Ferriday, seeking his cousin Jimmy Lee Swaggart.

Jimmy Lee supported his wife and three-year-old son by working as a dragline swamper. On weekends he preached. His daddy, Willie Leon, had given himself fully to the Lord and was the pastor of a little Pentecostal church in Wisner, some thirty miles north of Ferriday. Jimmy Lee was scheduled to preach at his daddy's church on the day of Jerry Lee's visit, and Jerry Lee agreed to accompany him to the service.

"Jerry Lee appeared to be his usual lighthearted self that morning," said Jimmy Lee Swaggart, looking back past twenty years to that remembered Sunday. "But later in church he was deeply affected by the Holy Spirit. His face turned ashen. He gripped the pew in front of him so tightly his knuckles turned white, shaking it as he wept and sobbed.

"A number of people moved forward that morning to receive the Lord and repent their sins. Jerry Lee remained in his seat, sobbing. Finally mama went over to pray with him and urge him to come forward. He always seemed to love her better than any of his aunts and uncles, and he hugged her neck emotionally. Yet he would not yield to the Holy Spirit's bidding."

After the service, Jerry Lee and Jimmy Lee stood outside the church and talked.

"I don't sing or play as well as you do," Jimmy Lee said, "but what little I have is God's. All of it. Just think what would happen if you gave Him all you had."

"I can't," Jerry Lee said. "I just can't."

Jerry Lee went to his Cadillac, drove away. A few weeks later, Jimmy Lee quit his job as a swamper and entered the ministry full-time. He preached his first revival in Sterlington, Louisiana, with Reverend Jewell Barton, the father of Jerry Lee's first wife, Dorothy. On the fourth night of the revival, Jimmy Lee fell sick with what doctors said was pneumonia, and he was hospitalized. "I listened to the radio during those days in the hospital," he later recalled in his autobiography. "The airwaves were filled with the heavy rock-'n'-roll beat of Jerry Lee's music. Dark, gloomy thoughts roamed through my mind. It seemed as if every demon in hell had crawled out to do battle with me. 'Look at Jerry Lee,' the voices said. 'He used to be a preacher but he got smart.' I cried out for God's help. Finally I reached over and picked up my Bible. It fell open to Joshua 1:9, 'Have not I commanded thee? Be strong and of a good courage; be not afraid, neither be thou dismayed: for the LORD thy God is with thee whithersoever thou goest.' God's healing power surged through my body. It was like fire in my veins. 'Jerry Lee can have "Great Balls of Fire,"' I declared, 'but I'll take the fire of the Holy Ghost! Hallelujah!' "

From here Jimmy Lee, like Jerry Lee, rose, but to fame and wealth of a different kind.

Over the Christmas holiday, Jerry Lee and Fats Domino headlined Alan Freed's twelve-day show at the Paramount Theatre in New York. The show, which also featured the Everly Brothers, Buddy Holly, Danny and the Juniors, and Paul Anka, broke the Paramount attendance record that had been set by Frank Sinatra fifteen years before. In his column, "On the Beat," *Billboard* reporter Ren Grevatt wrote:

> Really breaking it up for the Paramount audiences is Sun Records' phenomenal Jerry Lee Lewis. The Ferriday, La., rockabilly is one of the most dynamic chanters on the current scene, and according to Sam Phillips, chief of Sun: "He's the most sensational performer I've ever watched, bar none." This comes from the man who also developed Elvis Presley and Carl Perkins.

The same issue of *Billboard* reported that "Great Balls of Fire" had risen to Number 2 on the pop charts, Number 1 on the C & W charts, Number 5 on the R & B charts, Number 5 on the British charts, and that it was rising still.

But the best news of all that Christmas holiday was that Elvis had received his induction notice. Once Elvis entered the army, Jerry Lee would surely usurp the throne.

Returning to Memphis in January, 1958, Jerry Lee purchased a three-bedroom brick house at 4752 Dianne Street, about a mile south of the airport. The house cost him $12,000, which was little more than a good week's pay. He carried his lovely bride into the house, and they lived together in grandeur: Jerry Lee, Myra Gale, and a white poodle named Dinky.

Their neighbors on Dianne Street felt that the Lewises were a nice, quiet couple. But after an article appeared in the evening paper concerning Jerry Lee and Jane's ongoing divorce case, many of the neighbors began to suspect that there was something strange about the newlyweds in the pretty brick house, and they began to snoop. Eventually Jerry Lee paid a man $1,100 to erect a tall redwood fence around his property.

For his fourth single Jerry Lee recorded another song that had been written for him by Otis Blackwell called "Breathless." It was not as fine a song as "Great Balls of Fire." It was tame and gimmicky and inspired nothing of the Pentecostal power in Jerry Lee's voice.

Toward the end of January, Jerry Lee signed a contract to appear in the MGM movie *High School Confidential,* directed by Jack Arnold, who was well known for *The Creature from the Black Lagoon* and *The Incredible Shrinking Man.* The film starred Russ Tamblyn as a young narcotics agent working undercover at a California high school. Diane Jergens played a marijuana addict, and Jackie Coogan played a heroin dealer known as "Mr. A."

Jerry Lee collaborated on the film's title song with a young writer named Ronald J. Hargrave, and it was copyrighted in both their names on January 28. Jerry Lee cut the song at the Sun studio, then went to California, where the director set him, JW, Russ Smith, and their instruments in the bed of a pickup truck and had Jerry Lee lip-synch the song to a crowd of fake high school kids.

In early February Jerry Lee flew to Australia for five days of shows in Melbourne, Sydney, and Brisbane. Organized by Lee Gordon, an American promoter living in Australia, the tour also included Buddy Holly, Paul Anka, and the Australian pop star Johnny O'Keefe.

By the time he returned to Memphis, "Breathless" had been released and had sold about 100,000 copies. Dick Clark invited Jerry Lee to perform on the premiere of his prime-time ABC-TV show "The Dick Clark Show" on February 15. Wearing a black tuxedo with bright artificial leopard-skin lapels and piping, and refusing to lip-synch, Jerry Lee sang "Great Balls of Fire," then later closed the show with "Breathless." Several weeks later, Dick Clark and Judd Phillips were talking in the bar of the Manhattan Hotel. Each had a problem. Clark's problem was with his sponsor, Beechnut chewing gum: Mr. Norwood, the president of Beechnut, had been giving Clark a lot of heat, complaining that "The Dick Clark Show" was not selling enough gum. Judd's problem was with "Breathless": sales had tapered off because the song had a broken beat and was difficult to dance to.

"I could see the solution to both problems," Judd recalled. "I said, 'I'll tell you what we're gonna do, Dick. We'll tell the kids that if they send in fifty cents and five Beechnut wrappers, we'll send 'em a copy of "Breathless." ' There were bets all over ABC-TV that we'd fail. The first week we got fifty, maybe seventy-five orders. Next week, maybe five or six hundred. The third week, my God, fifty thousand! Truckloads of records! Lord, we had Sally, Sam, everybody packin' records.

We hadda cut it off in the end—the post office couldn't take it. And it turned out that this was the only time Beechnut ever outsold Wrigley's. One hell of a gimmick, yessir."

By the last week of March, "Breathless" was in the Top Ten of every chart—pop, C & W, and R & B—and "Great Balls of Fire" was still to be found on the pop and C & W charts.

On March 28 Jerry Lee flew to New York for the opening of Alan Freed's new package tour. Advertised as "The Big Beat," the show featured Jerry Lee, Chuck Berry, Buddy Holly, Frankie Lymon, the Chantels, and other well-known acts.

The tour began that Friday night at the Brooklyn Paramount. For over a year Jerry Lee had been adamant about closing every show he performed in. For more years Chuck Berry had been adamant in the same regard. Now they were about to play a show together, and they fought about who was to go on before whom. Alan Freed interceded and decided that Chuck Berry should close the show, since he had rock-'n'-roll seniority over Jerry Lee.

Jerry Lee did as he was bid that night; he went on before Chuck Berry. He had the crowd screaming and rushing the stage, and when it seemed that the screams had grown loudest and the rushing most chaotic, he stood, kicked the piano stool away with violence, and broke into "Great Balls of Fire." As the screaming chaos grew suddenly and sublimely greater, he drew from his jacket a Coke bottle full of gasoline, and he doused the piano with one hand as the other hand banged out the song; and he struck a wooden match and he set the piano aflame, and his hands, like the hands of a madman, did not quit the blazing keys, but kept pounding, until all became unknown tongues and holiness and fire, and the kids went utterly, magically berserk with the frenzy of it all; and Jerry Lee stalked backstage, stinking of gasoline and wrath, and he said to Chuck Berry, real calm, as the sound of the kids going crazy and stamping and yelling shook the walls; he said, "Follow that, nigger."

"Burned that damn piana to the ground," Jerry Lee said many years later, looking back on that Friday night in Brooklyn. "They forced me to do it, tellin' me I had to go on before Chuck."

After that night, Jerry Lee and Chuck Berry reached an understanding, and they came to be friends. The package tour was grueling: forty-six cities in forty-four days. On the morning of April 10, the "Today" show ran scenes of the previous night's "Big Beat" concert in Detroit. After seeing the image of Jerry Lee, Dave Garroway, the host of the "Today" show, shook his head in sincere confusion.

Trouble struck the tour at the start of its final week. After the May 3 show at the Boston Arena, gang fighting broke out in the streets. A nineteen-year-old sailor was stabbed, and at least fifteen other people were beaten, robbed, and raped in front of the Arena. The violence spread to other areas of the city. Packs of black-leather boys ran through the streets of Roxbury and Back Bay, looting stores and stabbing passersby. A pair of teenage girls attacked an older woman in the Dudley Street subway station and carved hate and obscenity into her soft arms with their switchblade knives.

Mayor John Hynes placed an immediate ban on any such future shows. Speaking with ire of "rock-'n'-roll paganism," District Attorney Garrett Byrne indicted Alan Freed under an old antianarchy statute. (These charges were eventually dropped, for the prosecution could not prove that Freed had intended to overthrow the government.) Following the trouble in Boston, mayors and police chiefs canceled "Big Beat" shows in Troy, New York, New Haven and New Britain, Connecticut, and Newark, New Jersey.

On the afternoon of May 13, a few days after Jerry Lee returned home to Memphis, Judge Harry Adams granted Jane Mitcham Lewis the divorce she sought. Called to the witness stand and asked about his present income, Jerry Lee testified that he had earned about $60,000 in record-sales royalties since January. Judge Adams awarded Jane $650 a month in alimony and $100 a month in child support. Jerry Lee sat quietly with his lawyer, Grover McCormick. He did not contest the judgment, nor did he mention that he had married Myra Gale Brown five months before.

Minutes after she left the Shelby County Court House, Jane told a lady reporter from the *Press-Scimitar* that she was still in love with Jerry Lee. "I'm going to try my hardest to get him back," she said. "I never went with anyone else but him. This divorce is partly his fault and partly my fault."

One of those who had testified against Jerry Lee at the trial was the ex-wife of Johnny Littlejohn, Jerry Lee's friend from the Blue Cat days. "I remember when Jane got that first alimony check," Johnny laughed. "She came down and celebrated at Hal's, some ol' club in Natchez."

Immediately after the trial, Jerry Lee drove to Ferriday, to visit his family and to be honored. The headline of the *Concordia Sentinel* that week was set in the seventy-two-point bold type that the paper usually used only for news of a major flood.

FERRIDAY SETS JERRY LEE LEWIS DAY SATURDAY
Mayor Will Present Key To City To
Rock 'n' Roll Singer

At two o'clock that Saturday afternoon, May 17, the Ferriday High School Band marched out of the Purvis Pontiac lot east down Louisiana Avenue. Riding high behind the brass band in an open Cadillac was Jerry Lee, flanked by Mayor W. D. Davis and Chamber of Commerce Manager C. A. Nelson.

Following the Cadillac proudly on foot were several hundred citizens, wearing clothes of toil and of worship, led by those teenagers who comprised the Jerry Lee Lewis Fan Club of Ferriday. The parade proceeded to the Ferriday radio station, KFNV, at 120 Louisiana Avenue, where Jerry Lee was interviewed on the air by Johnny Littlejohn, who had come to the station from WNAT not long after its start in 1956.

After the interview, the parade continued to the end of Louisiana Avenue, turned north on First Street, then west on Texas Avenue, halting at the Concordia Bank and Trust Company. There Jerry Lee was presented with a key to the city by Mayor Davis.

At nine o'clock that night, Jerry Lee performed at a benefit dance in the Ferriday High School gymnasium. From there he returned to Memphis. On the following Wednesday he was to embark on the most important tour of his career, and he wanted to rest.

GOLGOTHA

Oscar Davis: they called him the Baron. He was a coarse old man, a wily Nashville manager who had worked, at one time or another, with just about everyone who ever got rich singing with a Southern accent—from Hank Williams to Elvis Presley (whom he introduced to Colonel Tom Parker). It was Oscar Davis who, with the help of the William Morris Agency, devised Jerry Lee's trip to England—a thirty-seven-day tour consisting of thirty shows from which Jerry Lee was to return to America with $26,000 in his pocket, leaving in his wake a vastly expanded British market for his records.

All seemed to bode well as Jerry Lee sat and watched Myra Gale pack his rock-'n'-roll clothes for him. His new record, "High School Confidential," released little more than a week before, was already on the pop charts; and the movie was set to open in New York while he was away. "Breathless" had hit the Top Ten in England. Sun was about to issue his first long-playing album. And, best of all, Elvis was in the army, out of the way.

They left Memphis on Wednesday morning, May 21: Jerry Lee, Myra Gale, Russ Smith, JW and Lois Brown, Frankie Jean (whose husband had been drafted), and little Rusty Brown, Jerry Lee's three-year-old brother-in-law. They flew to New York and spent the night there awaiting Oscar Davis's arrival from Nashville. Judd Phillips was in New York on business, and he met with Jerry Lee in his hotel room.

Both Sam and Judd had advised that Jerry Lee keep his marriage to Myra Gale a secret. Now Judd asked Jerry Lee how he figured on introducing Myra to the press.

"She's my wife," Jerry Lee said. "There ain't nothin' wrong about that."

"Right an' wrong don't have anything to do with it," Judd said. "Those people ain't gonna like it."

"Look," declared Jerry Lee. "People want me, and they're gonna take me, no matter what."

"You're not gonna do like Sam and me think you should then, huh?"

"Hell no. Gotta do what's right."

Judd shook Jerry Lee's hand and wished him all the luck in the world; told him he'd see him in Memphis the next month.

They arrived at Heathrow Airport on the night of May 22. Jerry Lee and Myra stepped from the plane arm-in-arm and were set upon immediately by reporters and photographers from every London daily except the *Times*. They asked who she was, this smiling little girl in tight black slacks and a black-and-white blouse. Oscar Davis tried to distract them from her, but they would not be distracted.

"This is my wife, Myra," Jerry Lee said.

The reporters wanted to know how old she was.

"Fifteen," said Jerry Lee.

The reporters wanted to know how long they had been married.

"We were married two months ago, and we're very happy," said Jerry Lee.

The reporters wanted to know if this was his first marriage; when they were told that it was not, they wanted to know about the others.

"My first wife was named Dorothy," he said. "I was fifteen when I married her. She was seventeen. The marriage lasted only a year. My second wife was Jane. We were both sixteen when we married. It was a long marriage, lasted four years. We had a son called Jerry Lee. He's three now."

Then the reporters asked Myra if she didn't think that fifteen was too young an age at which to be married.

"Oh, no, not at all," Myra said. "Age doesn't matter back home. You can marry at ten if you can find a husband." Then the flashing lights blinded her, and she clung to her husband.

Oscar Davis drew Jerry Lee, Myra Gale, and the others away from the newsmen to waiting limousines. They were driven to the Westbury Hotel in Mayfair. Jerry Lee and Myra Gale checked into Room 127, the others into rooms farther down the hall.

The next day, Friday, Oscar Davis showed Jerry Lee a copy of the London *Daily Herald*. There was a large photo, taken at the airport the night before, of Jerry Lee and Myra Gale embracing, and in bold black letters the words

'ROCK' STAR'S WIFE IS 15
And It's His Third Marriage!

That same day, across the sea, Sam Phillips picked up a copy of the Memphis *Press-Scimitar* and inhaled slowly through his nostrils. The headline was: JERRY LEE LEWIS WEDS.

With Myra Gale in London.

After receiving news of the marriage from London, a Memphis reporter named Clark Porteous had done some digging, and now, in the *Press-Scimitar*, it was revealed that the marriage took place "almost exactly five months before Lewis was divorced by his second wife" and that "Myra's birth certificate reveals that she was born on July 11, 1944."

The day passed, then another, and Saturday night fell. The telephone in Jerry Lee's room rang. Myra Gale answered. It was Jane, calling to wish her ex-husband luck. She told Myra that she was still in love with Jerry Lee.

"But I'm living with him and you're not," Myra replied sweetly.

Jerry Lee and Myra were driven to the Regal Cinema in Edmonton, where the tour was to begin. Some two thousand British teenagers sat in a murmurous anticipation so perfect that it seemed to be orchestrated. The theatre lights dimmed and the Hedley Ward Trio, an English musical-comedy act, performed and were politely applauded. Then came the Treniers, the black jive-rock group led by the Alabama twins Claude and Clifford Trenier, now thirty-nine and fading from fame. They were applauded less politely, more enthusiastically. For minutes afterward there was nothing but the murmurous anticipation renewed.

Then there he was in a shocking-pink suit with sequined lapels and a black ribbon tie, the sort that Old Man Lewis had worn in those days before the wresting war, and he was beholding the audience while they beheld him from behind a blind of applause. He felt power, then loosened the grasp of his eyes and turned away toward where Myra stood in the wings. Russ Smith struck his stick to the chrome edge of his drum, and JW Brown struck his pick to the lowest string of his bass, and Jerry Lee Lewis raked the keys of the big piano and howled of the fire, and the audience, receiving the Devil's message variously, was no longer murmurous but wild with sound or silent, according to the bent of his or her soul.

Jerry Lee gave them little more than ten minutes—"he treats his audience with an attitude bordering on contempt," one British reporter wrote a few days later—and the teenagers, those who had been loud with excitement, those who had been silent, began to jeer and hiss as the curtain fell. Someone started to sing "God Save the Queen" and others joined in amid the jeering and hissing. Finally the curtain rose and Jerry Lee gave them more, gave it to them hard and frenzied and unrelenting, as a man who lay lustful and betrayed upon a hated wife; and then he left the stage.

On the following morning, Sunday, May 25, the *Daily Sketch* said that Jerry Lee "throws together everything that is bad in rock 'n' roll. Drooling at the piano, Lewis moans, grunts, wails and sneezes so close to the microphone he might be eating it." The front-page editorial in *The People* was more hostile, calling for all teenage subjects of the crown to boycott Jerry Lee's concerts and thus "show that even rock and roll hasn't entirely robbed them of their sanity." The editorial also urged the Home Secretary to have Jerry Lee immediately deported from the United Kingdom.

That afternoon a reporter from the *Daily Herald* crept into the Westbury Hotel and snake-tongued his way into Room 116, where he found Myra's mother, Lois. In his front-page story the next day the *Herald* reporter wrote, in his own italics, that, *"She lay in bed, nylon-nightie clad, smoothing her dark hair with one hand and holding a sheet close to her throat with the other."* Then, returning to Roman type: "'I'm horrified,' she said. 'Back in Memphis Jerry phoned Myra a lot. Then one night he said he was taking her to a movie. But they didn't go. They got married instead.'" The reporter proceeded to Room 122, where he found Oscar Davis, who *"came to the door wearing only*

Myra Gale with her brother, Rusty, and her mother, Clara Lois Brown, in London.

a pair of short pants." Finally he came to Room 127, Jerry Lee and Myra's room. "I knocked. Jerry answered: *'I can't come out. I haven't any clothes on.'*"

"Myra Gale and I couldn't have cared less," Frankie Jean recalled. "We were runnin' around, shoppin', drinkin' Cokes, eatin' ice cream."

That Sunday night Jerry Lee and Myra were driven to the Kilburn State Theatre in London for the second show of the tour. On the following day the *Herald* reported that only one thousand of the theater's four thousand seats were filled, adding that "Those who stayed away missed nothing."

On Monday night an editorial in the London *Evening Star* said that "Lewis should not be allowed to parade his charms before British teen-agers. He should be deported at once. He is an undesirable alien." Later that night, Jerry Lee performed at the Granada Theatre in Tooting, where he was met by cries of "Cradle-robber!" He beheld his audience, slowly drew the silver comb from the pocket of his yellow pants, and ran that comb back through his eight inches of fine blond waves, hair better by far, he knew, than any that his audience might ever possess; and when he did this, there were cries of "Sissy!"

He was scheduled to appear the following night at the Odeon Theatre in Birmingham. But that morning the British agent Leslie Grade, who had helped book the tour, met behind closed doors with the president of the Rank Organisation, which owned the theatres that Jerry Lee had been booked into for the rest of his long tour. After the meeting, Grade announced that the tour had been canceled. At 2:15 that afternoon, Jerry Lee, Myra Gale, Frankie Jean, Russ Smith, JW, Lois, and little Rusty left the Westbury Hotel through a side door, as Oscar Davis stayed behind to try to claim money from Leslie Grade and the Rank Organisation. Limousines carried them to the airport, where reporters and photographers were

The last night in England: Granada Theatre, Tooting, May 26, 1958.

Leaving London with his sister Frankie Jean and Myra Gale.

waiting. Leading Myra past them, Jerry picked up a paper at the airport newsstand and glanced at the headline, which proclaimed that France's new premier had averted civil war.

"Who's this de Gaulle guy?" he said loudly, as the newsmen caught up with him. "He seems to have gone over bigger than us." Then he hugged Myra and answered the reporters' questions.

One reporter wanted to know what Jerry Lee thought about the British.

"You British are nice, on the whole," he said, looking into the man's eyes. "But some of y'all are jealous, just plain jealous."

Another reporter wanted to know if Jerry Lee thought that the scandal might hurt his career.

"Back in America, I got two lovely homes, three Cadillacs, and a farm." Then he squeezed Myra's hand and said, "What else could anyone want?"

A Pan American plane carried Jerry Lee and Myra and the sighing others away from that great isle, that isle from which their ancestors had been carried almost two hundred years before. Jerry Lee put a stick of gum in his mouth and looked down at the ocean. He kept looking at it as he chewed the gum.

The sky was overcome by twilight. The ocean turned gold, then filled with all the darkling stained-glass glimmerings in the world. As he chewed his gum and beheld it, Jerry Lee Lewis knew that its sadness was as great and immense as its power; and that his mother was waiting on the other side. He turned away from the ocean toward his wife. He kissed the clove-brown hair that curled softly at her temple, then he closed his eyes and recommenced chewing his gum.

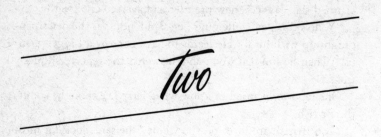

Two

As the airplane headed toward Idlewild Airport in New York, the United Kingdom celebrated the success of its exorcism. Under the headline BABY–SNATCHER QUITS, the London *Daily Herald* gloatingly reported in its Wednesday edition that "The Jerry Lee Lewis circus flew sadly out of London last night twelve hours after two big British theatre circuits had stopped his five-week rock 'n' roll tour."

Upon landing at Idlewild on Wednesday morning, Jerry Lee found that what waited for him was almost as bad as what he had left behind. As the crowd of reporters came toward Jerry Lee, Myra ran into a private Pan American waiting-room. Photographers flooded Jerry Lee's vision with white flashing.

"I'm sorry I didn't wear my rock-'n'-roll suit for you guys," is all he said. He was dressed in a gray tweed jacket.

A reporter from the *New York Post* asked Jerry Lee if it was true that he had been deported.

"I wasn't deported," he said calmly. "It's just that the English don't react to rock 'n' roll like Americans. They don't scream. They just clap. I like screaming myself. I guess you can say I just got homesick."

Myra Gale was brought from the waiting-room. She clung to her husband's side. Someone asked her what she thought of it all.

"I think what Jerry thinks about it," she said.

A reporter from the *Daily News* asked Jerry Lee if he didn't think it was a bit odd for a man to marry a thirteen-year-old girl.

"You can put this down," he said, raising his voice for the first time. "She's a woman."

Jerry Lee, Myra, and the rest did not stay in New York for the debut of *High School Confidential,* which was to open Friday at the Loew's State in Times Square. Instead they boarded a Capital Airlines plane and were home in Memphis a few minutes after two in the afternoon. At the Memphis airport they once again found that reporters and photographers awaited them, and that these reporters and these photographers were no more kind than those in London and in New York. In a story that appeared in the next day's edition of the *Press-Scimitar,* one reporter who had greeted Jerry Lee at the airport commented that "Fans don't crowd about the Lewis home on Dianne as they do around Elvis Presley's place."

Sun Records' response to the situation was not much better than that of the press. Within seven days of Jerry Lee's arrival in Memphis, Sun released a novelty record called "The Return of Jerry Lee." Contrived by Jack Clement, the record consisted of a series of questions spoken by Memphis disc jockey George Klein and answered by snatches of Jerry Lee's previous records. At one point Clement had Klein ask, "What did Queen Elizabeth say about you?" After that question, Clement spliced in

Jerry Lee singing the words "Goodness gracious! Great balls of fire!"

Thinking that it might placate the press, Jerry Lee decided to remarry Myra in a ceremony of impeccable legality. On the weekend after returning to Memphis, Jerry Lee and Myra Gale drove south to Ferriday. They filled out a marriage license at the parish courthouse in Vidalia. Since Jerry Lee's last Louisiana marriage, more than six years before, something new had been added to the license form, and Jerry Lee filled this new thing out with a quickness and an audacity that brought a smile to the face of Uncle Lee Calhoun:

Relation of Bride to Groom: NONE

A few days later, on the afternoon of June 4, Jerry Lee and Myra were rewed by a Methodist minister at the house Jerry Lee had bought for his parents in Ferriday. Mamie and Aunt Stella threw rice, Elmo and Uncle Lee nodded.

Jerry Lee and Sam Phillips paid for a full page in *Billboard,* and the following open letter appeared in the June 9 issue of that magazine.

Dear Friends:

I have in recent weeks been the apparent center of a fantastic amount of publicity and of which none has been good.

But there must be a little good even in the worst people, and according to the press releases originating in London, I am the worst and am not even deserving of one decent press release.

Now this whole thing started because I tried and did tell the truth. I told the story of my past life, as I thought it had been straightened out and that I would not hurt anybody in being man enough to tell the truth.

I confess that my life has been stormy. I confess further that since I have become a public figure I sincerely wanted to be worthy of the decent admiration of all the people, young and old, that admired or liked what talent (if any) I have. That is, after all, all that I have in a professional way to offer.

If you don't believe that the accuracy of things can get mixed up when you are in the public's eye, then I hope you never have to travel this road I'm on.

There were some legal misunderstandings in this matter that inadvertently made me look as though I invented the word indecency. I feel I, if nothing else, should be given credit for the fact that I have at least a little common sense and that if I had not thought the legal aspects of this matter were not completely straight, I certainly would not have made a move until they were.

I did not want to hurt Jane Mitcham, nor do I want to hurt my family and children. I went to court and did not contest Jane's divorce actions, and she was awarded $750.00 a month for child support and alimony. Jane and I parted from the courtroom as friends and as a matter of fact, chatted before, during and after the trial with no animosity whatsoever.

In the belief that for once my life was straightened out, I invited my mother and daddy and little sister to make the trip to England. Unfortunately, mother and daddy felt that the trip would be too long and hard for them and didn't go, but sister did go along with Myra's little brother and mother.

I hope that if I am washed up as an entertainer it won't

be because of this bad publicity, because I can cry and
wish all I want to, but I can't control the press or the
sensationalism that these people will go to to get a scandal started to sell papers. If you don't believe me, please
ask any of the other people that have been victims of the
same.

Sincerely,
Jerry Lee Lewis

Still the press would not relent. In its "Newsmakers" section, in an item captioned "Alpha and Omega," *Newsweek* reported the more lurid details of Jerry Lee's expulsion from
England, juxtaposing the report with the news that milk-
drinking Pat Boone had recently graduated from Columbia
University magna cum laude. In the *New York Herald Tribune*
columnist Hy Gardner remarked that "The Jerry Lee Lewises
are going to have an addition to the family. He bought her a
new doll."

Even old friends had forsaken him. While Jerry Lee was still
in London, Dick Clark had received a phone call at three in the
morning.

"Dick," the caller had said, "you know who this is but don't
say anything. I just want to tell you to watch out. Jerry Lee
Lewis married his thirteen-year-old cousin and all hell's gonna
break loose."

Clark later recalled with remorse that "In a very cowardly
act I decided to hold off further bookings for Jerry Lee on the
show, for which I've been sorry ever since."

On June 11 Jerry Lee made his first New York nightclub
appearance, at the Cafe de Paris, a new club owned by impre-
sario Lou Walters. Jerry Lee and Myra arrived in New York a
day early and checked into a suite at the Edison Hotel, to com-

At the Cafe de Paris, New York City, June 10, 1958.

ply with Oscar Davis's request that Jerry Lee hold a press conference on the eve of the opening, to assuage the lingering hostility. One of those who attended the press conference was the columnist Hy Gardner, who commented that Jerry Lee's music possessed "the contagious, almost frightening beat of a tribal drummer."

"Y'know," Jerry Lee said to him, "all that stuff about rock 'n' roll incitin' to riot is trash. Music didn't do it. It had to come out somewhere. But, anyway, I'm not a rocker. I'm a boogie-woogie man."

Opening night at the Cafe de Paris did not go well. A month before, Jerry Lee had been able to fill great auditoriums and arenas. But the Cafe de Paris was not filled that night, and many of those who came had the look in their eyes that Jerry Lee had seen as a boy in the eyes of farmers who stood waiting to enter a tent at the Concordia Parish Fair, a tent wherein an old man stood shaking and reeking of cheap whiskey and prepared to bite off the head of a squawking hen and swallow that small bleeding head in one shuddering gulp. Jerry Lee failed to return to the Cafe de Paris the following night as he had been scheduled to. Instead, he returned to the South, to the land of his ancestors.

The summer passed, but trouble did not. On the first day of fall, Elvis, whose kingship Jerry Lee had dreamed to usurp, sailed in khaki to Germany. Before his departure, a reporter at the Brooklyn Army Terminal asked Elvis how he felt about what had befallen Jerry Lee.

"He's a great artist," Elvis said, shifting from his left hand to his right a book called *Poems That Touch the Heart.* "I'd rather not talk about his marriage, except that if he really loves her I guess it's all right."

Not long after arriving in Germany, Elvis met and fell in love with a fourteen-year-old girl named Priscilla Beaulieu. He

Memphis, June, 1958.

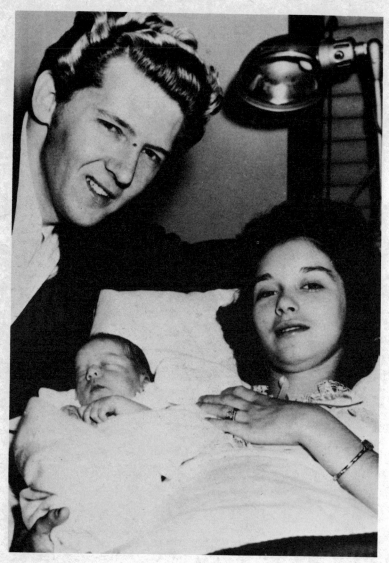

With newborn Steve Allen Lewis at Ferriday Hospital.

eventually brought her to live with him at Graceland, keeping her, carefully, quietly, waiting till 1967 to marry her without taint.

By the time Elvis sailed for Germany, Myra Gale knew that she was pregnant. On the morning of February 27, 1959, a few weeks after the plane crash that killed Buddy Holly, the Big Bopper, and Ritchie Valens, Myra Gale gave birth in Ferriday to a seven-pound boy child. Later in the day Jerry Lee decided to name his second son Steve Allen Lewis, in honor of one of the few decent men he had met outside of Concordia Parish.

Soon Jerry Lee moved his family into a new home at 5042 East Shore Drive, out near Coro Lake. It was a fine ranch-style house with four bedrooms, a large patio, and a swimming pool. Jerry Lee would sit by the pool in the early evening, at that hour when the sun began to fall and the darkling, sighing colors came. He would sit there and not smile and not think. It was only a matter of time, he knew, till he would once again be redeemed. He would sit there, gazing at the tame, purling water, and he would know that. And he would make a fist, wishing that there were a horse that he could knock to its fucking knees.

MAMMON

One

He rested one hand on the cold porcelain urinal, steadying himself. From where he stood he could see the upraised seat of a flooded commode. There were four small knobs on the underside of the seat and the paint was chipped, exposing old wood. It looked to him like the face of a lying Chinee. He snorted, almost smiling, then lowered his head.

He was somewhere in Minneapolis, and it was Easter Sunday, 1962. All was not well. Since that ruinous summer of 1958, there had been no more big hits, no more big paychecks. But still he pumped onward, roaming the country in a dirty Cadillac, howling of the fire and of the shaking, seeking his own vague salvation, indomitable. In less than a week from this Easter Sunday he was to fly across the sea to tour England—that place he had neither seen nor missed in four years—and he knew not what to expect. He was no longer the contender to the throne of the kingdom of rock 'n' roll. Things were different now, strange and unreal, like the lying Chinee he almost beheld in this dank, once-white chamber somewhere in Minneapolis. Elvis reigned in solitude now, no longer performing in public, withdrawing into a mystery commensurate with his sovereignty. Rock 'n' roll itself had changed. It was soft and weak, and whenever Jerry Lee heard it on the radio it did not remind him of Haney's Big House, or of the Assembly of God, or of anything, except perhaps injustice. At times it seemed to him that only he himself was rocking on, burning true after all these years. But his fame had dwindled, and so had his purse. He had once played for thousands of dollars a night; now he played for hundreds. He continued to make records for Sun, and many of those records were fine, but Sun itself was barely there anymore; it had begun to fall apart not long after Jerry Lee's return from England. That summer of 1958 Judd departed to start his own company, Judd Records, in Sheffield, Alabama; not long after that, Johnny Cash, then Carl Perkins, left Sun and signed with Columbia; early in 1959 Sam fired Jack Clement for "insubordination"; and the advertisements that Sam put in *Billboard* to announce Jerry Lee's new records kept getting smaller and smaller. A year ago, it had seemed that Jerry Lee's luck was about to change. His version of the 1959 Ray Charles hit "What'd I Say" had broken into the pop charts and risen to Number 30. It had crossed to the C & W and R & B charts, had even broken into the Top Ten in England. However, the record had fallen quickly. A few months later, his recording of Hank Williams's "Cold, Cold Heart" had been a small country hit. But since then there had been nothing.

Things had changed within Jerry Lee's own family, too. His aunt, Jimmy Lee Swaggart's mama, Minnie Bell, had died on a June day in 1960. She had been only forty-three. Jerry Lee had been one of the pallbearers, delivering her to her place in the Calhoun dirt in the little cemetery near Clayton. Jerry Lee's teenage sister Frankie Jean had borne a child, and that child, too, now lay in Uncle Lee's dirt. And Elmo and Mamie, after more than thirty years of marriage, years encompassing flood and drought, hunger and plenty, birth and death, had separated in the fall of 1961.

Yes, it seemed to Jerry Lee, as he flushed the urinal and raised his head—yes, it had become strange and unreal, all of it.

Nine hundred miles away, in Memphis, as dusk settled on that Sunday of resurrection, Myra Gale sat at the kitchen table making a grocery list. Little Steve Allen, who had turned three in February, pulled at her skirt for attention. She reached out and rubbed his blond crew cut. She finished the list and looked at the clock on the kitchen wall. It was 6:40; there was still time to get to the store. Then she noticed that Stevie was gone. She searched the house, calling his name, and the farther she searched and did not find him, the faster and harder her heart shook beneath her breast. Old Elmo was on the porch, having himself a drink, and Myra Gale roused him to join in the search. Finally, as the sound of her heart filled her ears to the exclusion of all other sounds, she ran to her next-door neighbor, a man named E. E. Haning, and in a voice of terror she asked him to search the pool behind her house.

The man ran to the pool and jumped into the shallow end, then walked slowly toward the depths, forty feet away. The pool was murky and unrevealing, thick with algae and the dead, sodden leaves of a past season. In about five feet of water, near a little ladder at the edge of the pool, the neighbor met a soft, horrible, gently drifting weight. He raised the tiny body and, trembling, laid it on the concrete patio. Myra felt something that she had never known to exist, and she came apart in shock.

Volunteers from the Whitehaven Fire Department crowded around the little corpse and attempted to give it mouth-to-mouth resuscitation. Then a doctor who lived nearby arrived, without his bag. He stuck a penknife into Stevie's breast and tore downward, then pulled the jagged-rent sternum apart, exposing the heart. He massaged it for many minutes, then stood sighing, shaking his head. He dipped his hands into the pool and rinsed the blood from them.

Jerry Lee arrived in Memphis the following morning. He stood sorrowed at the edge of that fancy cement pool that Mammon gold had bought, and he looked into the dismal killing water with eyes that were the enemy of all joy and all hope. He called across the sea to London and told of what had befallen him, and he tried to postpone the scheduled tour. The man in London told him that no such arrangements could be made.

Jerry Lee drove to the National Funeral Home and claimed the corpse of his son, then drove south to Ferriday. At the little white Assembly of God Church the next day, a preacher stood before the small casket and told of many things. Then, when the afternoon sun was bright, Jerry Lee placed his boy to rest in the little cemetery near Clayton. He ordered a tombstone for the grave, and he told the man that he wanted a little lamb atop the stone—a little lamb exactly like that that watched in silence over the nearby grave of the brother that Jerry Lee had never truly known—and this was done.

On Saturday, five days after burying his son, Jerry Lee arrived in London. That Sunday night, April 29, in Newcastle, he sang for a British audience for the first time since 1958. He sang with vengeance and with sadness and with the power of the Holy Ghost, and those people in Newcastle, they loved him, and the people who heard him the following night, they loved him, too. On Tuesday he called Myra Gale and told her to join him. A few days later, on May 7, she flew to London,

A little stone lamb near Clayton.

striding past the few photographers and reporters who awaited her, striding as if to tell them that she was now seventeen—almost eighteen, really; that she was still married to the man of her dreams, and that she was strong.

The tour went well, but not long after Jerry Lee came back home things were worse than they had been. The death of his son bore heavily on his heart, and new and terrible demons clutched his neck and filled his lungs with their unthinkable, sinful breath.

He had always been strict with Myra. Since adolescence, she had been shaped like soft clay within his hands. Frankie Jean remembers that Jerry Lee dictated what clothes Myra wore, and he dictated these clothes according to the precepts of the Pentecostal Church. He did not allow her to wear any makeup or to cut her hair. He told her which records she might listen to, which television programs she might watch, which books

The return to London, May, 1962.

she might read. (Once he had caught her with a paperback copy of Erskine Caldwell's *Tobacco Road,* the 1932 bestseller in which an older man marries a twelve-year-old white-trash girl. Jerry Lee tore the book from her and censured her mightily.) Myra, who knew little of the world, simply believed that all marriages were like her own, and she bent her knee in diffident fealty.

Still, he smelled a sinfulness in her. Women had thrown themselves on him for five years. Wherever he went, it seemed, cheap-perfumed thighs parted, lithe and yielding as the windblown reeds of Turtle Lake—had parted first to receive whatever scrap of garish, stinking fame and glory they might, then later to receive the grotesque wraith of that fame and that glory. Every time he disgorged himself in the mouth of whoredom, he cursed all women for what they had to him shown themselves to be. He turned on his wife, unable to believe or to see that she could be any different from the rest. He accused her of adultery, and he beat her. Perhaps his mother, who often stayed with the couple in Memphis, encouraged her dear son's accusations; for she, in motherhood, trusted none of Jerry Lee's wives, believing that they lusted only for his gold, and she spent time seeking to discover Myra Gale in an act of moist indiscretion.

Now a demon, or demons, inspired Jerry Lee to make accusations of a new sort. He began to imply that little Stevie's death was a punishment for Myra Gale's sins. In the past Myra had obeyed her husband's command that she attend church regularly (though he himself attended very rarely), but this new accusation brought a chill to Myra's teenage soul, and she ran to the Holy Spirit for comfort, praying no longer in mere obedience but rather in heartfelt need. A preacher at the Church of God on Highway 61 told Myra Gale that the Holy Spirit could bring the dead back to life. For almost two years following this revelation, she besought the Holy Ghost to breathe miraculous life into her dead son, to wrench him from beneath Lee Calhoun's awful dirt and deliver him into her arms. She took to the pulpit and declared her love for the Almighty, as her husband all the while derided her for her blasphemous hypocrisy. When she was twenty and the Holy Ghost had given her no sign, she unclasped her hands, cut her hair, and wept. By then she had borne new life, a seven-pound blond, blue-eyed girl, who came into the world on August 30, 1963, while Jerry Lee was out of town pumping piano in Hot Springs, Arkansas. The child received the name Phoebe Allen Lewis and was placed in a pink layette.

On the May 6 prior to Phoebe's birth, Jerry Lee embarked on his second successful tour of Great Britain. Returning home a little less than five weeks later, on June 6, he was asked by a reporter from the *Press-Scimitar* if his audiences abroad compared him with Elvis.

"I really wish people would stop tryin' to compare me with Elvis," Jerry Lee sternly responded. "We are entirely different performers. 'Bout the only thing we got in common is that we're from Tennessee." Then his voice was more easy, and he almost grinned, saying, "Of course, Elvis has made a lot more money than I have. But, then, he had a three-year head start."

For the second year in a row, Jerry Lee had driven crowds wild across the sea; but in his homeland he continued to drift into the shadows. On the hot summer nights of July 27–28, 1963, he went into the Sun studio at 639 Madison, the new, four-track studio that Sam Phillips had opened two years before, shuttering the original, haunted studio on Union Avenue, where Elvis, Carl Perkins, Jerry Lee, and the rest had worked their redneck wonders in the decade past. On those two July nights, Jerry Lee recorded eight songs. Some of these, such as "Invitation to Your Party" and "One Minute Past Eternity," were new songs, written by Sun writer Bill Taylor. Others were old, such as Hoagy Carmichael's 1939 "Hong Kong Blues" and James Bland's "Carry Me Back to Old Virginny," which dated to 1878, to the days of Leroy Lewis's boyhood. (Ray Charles had cut the song in 1960, but in the slow, traditional way; Jerry Lee turned the song into a fast, hard boogie.) These were the last songs that Jerry Lee recorded for Sun. When he left the studio sometime between ten and midnight that Sunday night, Sam Phillips and his legendary little record company lost the final piece of glory that remained of the magic fifties. Sun lingered, and Sam continued to release Jerry Lee's records till as late as the spring of 1965, when he issued "Carry Me Back to Old Virgina." (Altogether, Jerry Lee had cut more than one hundred sixty titles during his years at Sun.) Then, in 1968, the lingering ceased, and Sam Phillips receded into the great wealth he had acquired, not as the president of Sun but as an original shareholder in Holiday Inns, Inc., which had been founded in Memphis in 1952, the same year that Sam had started Sun.

Jerry Lee's contract with Sun legally expired on September 6, 1963. Frank Casone, whom Jerry Lee had taken on as his manager in July, announced that Jerry Lee had signed a five-year deal with Smash, the new, Nashville-based subsidiary of Mercury Records. (Casone, whose contract entitled him to 25 percent of the Killer's income, was also the owner of the Oriental, a Memphis nightclub where Jerry Lee often played. Above the entrance of the club was a twenty-foot neon image of Jerry Lee with flashing hair and fingers.) On September 22, with producer Shelby Singleton, the thirty-year-old Texan who had signed him to Smash, Jerry Lee went into the Phillips Recording Studio on 17th Avenue South in Nashville. (This was the studio, opened by Sam Phillips in early 1961, where Jerry Lee had cut "What'd I Say" and "Cold, Cold Heart," his last mildly successful records.) The first Smash sessions were devoted largely to new versions of Jerry Lee's early Sun records, such as "Whole Lotta Shakin' Goin' On," "Great Balls of Fire," and "Breathless." Also cut were a speeded-up rendition of "Hit the Road, Jack," which had been one of Ray Charles's biggests hits, and a song called "Pen and Paper," written by Eddie Kilroy, a Texas rodeo rider who knew both Jerry Lee and Shelby Singleton and who had lived and worked with Mickey Gilley in Houston. These two songs comprised Jerry Lee's first Smash single, while the reworkings of the Sun material were made into an album, *The Golden Hits of Jerry Lee Lewis*. Both the single and the album were released in November. The album began to sell, slowly, steadily, and by March 1964 it appeared at the bottom of the LP charts; but it rose only to Number 116, then quickly fell. The single did worse, failing even to make the charts.

Early in 1964 Jerry Lee made another successful tour of England and the Continent, where he recorded a live album at the Star Club in Hamburg. Though the album sold well in Germany and France, legal problems stood in the way of its release in America. Back home, Jerry Lee returned to the studio; but it seemed that no Holy Ghost dwelt in Nashville. His second Smash single, "I'm on Fire" (co-written by Richard Gottehrer, who went on to produce Blondie in the seventies), appeared in the Number 98 position on the pop charts for one week, in April, 1964, then vanished. The next record, "She Was My Baby," did not even break into the bottom of the charts. The fourth Smash single, a version of "High Heel Sneakers," recorded live at the Birmingham Municipal Auditorium on July 1, hit the Number 91 position on the pop charts the week before Thanksgiving, but was gone the following week.

After performing a benefit for the Westwood School PTA in Memphis on November 17, Jerry Lee flew across the sea, to be once again worshipped and adored by those who had brought about his downfall. On the day of his arrival in London, he took part in the filming of *Be My Guest,* a low-budget pop musical directed by Lance Comfort and starring David Hemmings as a teenage reporter out to expose a rigged talent contest in Brighton. Jerry Lee's part in the film was restricted to a performance of "My Baby Don't Love No One But Me," during which he was backed by the Nashville Teens, the British group who had played with him at the Star Club earlier in the year. The movie was released and distributed the following year by Rank, the organization that had canceled Jerry Lee's 1958 tour.

The next day, before a taping of the TV show "Ready, Steady, Go!," a reporter from *Melody Maker* inquired as to the current state of Jerry Lee's career.

"I'm workin'," Jerry Lee answered, drawing on a fat cigar. "I'm workin', and I'll keep workin'. I'll play dance halls, clubs. I'll do TV, movies. I'll work any way I can get it, as long as it's decent."

On this tour Jerry Lee saw that something strange was going on. Boys were dressing funny—not in the familiar teddy boy clothes, but in stripes and polka dots and silly little caps. And the girls, too: white boots and skirts that barely covered the source of all sorrow. And they all, all of them, boys and girls together, had the same hair—not true fine long hair like his own, but hair so straight that it seemed to be steam-ironed, and clipped across the brow in bangs, like dobbin ponies. And everywhere that music—that goddamn, motherfucking music. He had figured that those Beatle boys, whom he had met on his last trip, would be gone by now, gone. But not only were they not gone, they were bigger than ever; and there were whole new bunches of them, like those Rolling Stone boys, duded up like nigger faggots on the last night of Mardi Gras—and getting rich, all of them, every last motherfucking one of them. And there he was, Jerry Lee Lewis, better than all of them, all of them put together, and he could not even get him a hit, not one stray hit.

He got on that plane and he rode back to America, to where men, even if they could not recognize a good hit record when they heard one, were men, and women, whores or no, kept covered in public those parts that only their rightful husbands and the Holy Ghost had ought to see. But when he reached New York he noticed that a lot of the boys looked like those boys in London and that a lot of the girls' skirts were much shorter than he seemed to recall—and he heard those Beatles coming from out a radio. When he got to Memphis, he saw that even there some of that dobbin hair had begun to sprout. And right after Christmas, when he went to Los Angeles to be on that new TV show, that "Shindig," it seemed that he and Willie Nelson were the only two normal-looking people backstage. But he went on out there, and he howled, and he sang "Mean Woman Blues" and "Whole Lotta Shakin' Goin' On," and by the time he was done everybody was stark wild, and Jack Good, the man who had hired him for the show, ran over to him and signed him up for five more appearances; and as he was signing the paper, Jerry Lee knew that he had something that the Beatles did not have—something that was powerful even without the stinking cape of fame—and he knew that he would be around long after the Beatles were gone. Then he went out and had his hair cut, the hair that six and seven years ago had been the longest and finest in the world; he had it cut good and short, and he looked in the Bible, in I Corinthians, and he found where it said, "Doth not even nature itself teach

you, that, if a man have long hair, it is a shame unto him";
and he poured him a good one and he called up Myra Gale and
told her that he loved her.

He traveled to Nashville on the first Tuesday in January of
1965 for three days of sessions at the Fred Foster Studio. These
sessions, at which Jerry Lee cut Pentecostal versions of old rock
classics, went well; but no hits were to come of them. Two
weeks later, he was saddened to hear that Alan Freed, dis-
graced and broke, forgotten, had died on January 20 of uremia
at age forty-two.

Lost and fading in the midst of those strange days, Jerry Lee
did not lose faith in the power within himself. But he had no
way of knowing that a journey across a terrible desert had just
begun or of what awaited him on the other side.

Two

He had drunk and taken pills since he was a teenager pumping piano in the Natchez honky-tonks; but he had allowed neither the liquor nor the pills to reign over him. Since the death of his son, however, he had grown more extreme, and whiskey and drugs were fast becoming as important a part of his life as God and music. The booze and the pills stirred the hell within him and made him to utter hideous peals. At times he withdrew into his own shadow, brooding upon all manner of things—abominable, unutterable, and worse. At times he stalked and ranted in proud and foul omnipotence, commanding those about him as Belial his minions. He was the Killer and he was immortal—damned to be, for as long as there were good and evil to be torn between in agony. He would sit backstage in a thousand dank nightclubs, and he would know this, and he would swallow more pills and wash them down with three fingers more of whiskey, and he would know it even more. He would walk like a man to the stage, with his Churchill in one hand and his water glass of whiskey in the other, and he would pound the piano and sing his sinful songs, and he would beckon those before him, mortals, made not as he to destruction from the womb; he would beckon them to come, to stand with him awhile at the brink of hell. Then he would be gone into the ancient night, to more pills and more whiskey, to where the black dogs never ceased barking and dawn never broke; he would go there.

By 1965 he had begun to take on the aspects of one of those men in his daddy's tales. He spoke with a voice much older than his thirty years, and he quoted frequently from the darker passages of Scripture. He drank straight from the bottle and smoked the biggest cigars he could find. He bragged of his indestructibility, and he accumulated arms of all manner— pearl-handled pistols and long, sleek heavy-assault guns. He surrounded himself with kin and idolators, those who would sit in diffident reverence as he preached of God and Mammon, would perform for him his errands of perdition, and would regard him as a god, inviolable and right.

He drew his past into the present to assuage the darkness. In the spring of 1964 he had broken his management contract with Frank Casone and hired instead Cecil Harrelson, his boyhood friend from Ferriday. In 1963 Jerry Lee had brought his fifteen-year-old sister, Linda Gail, into the Sun studio and recorded a duet with her, a George Jones song called "Seasons of My Heart." Since then Linda Gail's ambitions as a singer had grown, and Jerry Lee had carried her. After his first, successful performance on the ABC-TV show "Shindig," Jerry Lee showed up for his second appearance, on February 17, with seventeen-year-old Linda Gail in tow. On May 5 (three weeks after Jerry Lee had closed his third "Shindig" performance with a sanctified rendition of "Take Me Out to the Ball

Game"), Linda Gail sang on the program without her famous brother. This led to her being hired as a member of the touring "Shindig" show and to her first solo record, "Small Red Diary," which was released by ABC-Paramount in the spring of 1965. (The record was produced by Felton Jarvis, who would take over as Elvis's producer the following year.) After the "Shindig" road show disbanded, after the record failed, Linda Gail returned to Jerry Lee, recording a duet with him in September and traveling around the country with him, serving sometimes as an opening act, and eventually proving to possess as great a propensity toward marriage as the brother she worshipped.

By the end of 1965, Jerry Lee's band had become as notorious for their excesses as he and seemed to be doing their best to keep pace with their boss in the pursuit of self-annihilation. Their first big bust occurred on October 11 of that year, little more than a week after Jerry Lee's thirtieth birthday.

Following a show in Grand Prairie, Texas, police surrounded Jerry Lee's Cadillac as it pulled into the motel where he and the band were staying. Jerry Lee was not in the car, but in another car, following. The police searched the Cadillac and found 157 white tablets and 45 green tablets beneath the back seat and immediately arrested those who had been in the car: bass player Herman "Hawk" Hawkins, age thirty-three; guitarist Charles "Red Man" Freeman, age twenty-three; drummer Robert "Tarp" Tarrant, age twenty-two; and a teen-age girl from nearby Irving who had been picked up at the show. Though most of the pills found belonged to Jerry Lee, he was not arrested.

These three men were Jerry Lee's band in the autumn of 1965. Hawk Hawkins ended up in a bitter lawsuit against Jerry Lee. Charlie Freeman ended up dead at the age of thirty-one. And Tarp Tarrant ended up in the Memphis penitentiary.

Robert Morris Tarrant, the grandson of a Baptist minister,

had been born in Adel, Georgia, on May 21, 1943. Joining Jerry Lee's band, for thirty dollars a week, in 1960 (when JW Brown, Jerry Lee's father-in-law, was the band's only other member), Tarrant, in 1965 and for many years thence, was both the youngest member of the band and, having been with the band longer than anyone else, the member with the most seniority. He was also, by the time of the 1965 bust, dwelling in the shadow of death.

"It got out of hand," Tarp Tarrant, Number 82707, recalled, imprisoned now—perhaps regretting his days with Jerry Lee—but nonetheless saved, for within the walls of the Memphis penitentiary he has found his way back to Christ. "With Jerry Lee it got to the point where he didn't try to hide it anymore, and he didn't try to do it in proportion. Never enough of nothin', that's the way it was. It got worse and worse, and he started havin' a lot of goons around. They were buyin' him dope, and, of course, they were totin' dope, too. They were totin' a lot of money for him, 'cause everything was always cash with Jerry. Guns. Hell, man, we had guns galore.

"Sometime after that bust in Grand Prairie, I started havin' what you might call a nervous breakdown. I had been doin' speed real heavy, drinkin' real heavy. I was gettin' real sick, real weak. I was down to about a hundred and ten pounds, eatin' pills like they were popcorn. I knew when I took a certain pill and drank certain stuff with it, I knew what kind of pain I was gonna have. I knew what I was headin' for every time I did it.

"It was either Des Moines, Iowa, or Dayton, Ohio. I was twenty-two years old, alone in a motel room. I was havin' a lot of pains. I had the shakes. I was heavin' a lot of blood. I started cryin', and I fell to my knees and started prayin', and I asked God to help me. And there was Christ. I felt better immediately. I felt clean, I felt good.

Howling in Babylon, with Tarp Tarrant at the drums, 1963.

"It was like the first time I took LSD. I wanted to go right out and turn the world on. I wanted to turn the world on to Christ. I was very overwhelmed with the feeling of happiness that I'd got. But that time didn't last but about three or four months."

The journey through the desert continued, and none fell. Pistols were fired, bottles broken, pianos ruined, lives cursed, handcuffs locked and loosed, but no one fell, either from want of water or of shrieking Azazel. Pale and shaken, with a lighted cigar, a half-full bottle, a handful of pills, and the benison of the Holy Ghost, Jerry Lee Lewis neared the edge of the desert. It was 1967, and hardly anyone outside of Concordia Parish knew who he was.

Three

The record company had tried everything. In May, 1965, Shelby Singleton had taken Jerry Lee to Mirasound Studios in New York City, searching for a new sound. The single that had resulted from that New York session, a version of Huey Smith's "Rockin' Pneumonia and the Boogie-Woogie Flu," certainly possessed a new sound—at Singleton's request, Jerry Lee had performed the song on a harpsichord—but, like all the Smash singles before it, it failed to sell. In January and February, 1966, Singleton had reunited Jerry Lee with Jack Clement for a series of sessions at the Sun studio in Memphis, but again, nothing. In May, 1967, after Shelby Singleton left Smash, Jerry Lee's new producer, twenty-six-year-old, Louisiana-born Jerry Kennedy, had tried leaving the keyboard out altogether. The resulting single, "It's a Hang-Up, Baby," went unnoticed.

Eddie Kilroy had been working as the national promotion

manager of MGM Records during the week and rodeoing on weekends. One Saturday afternoon he was thrown from a bull and his back was broken. He was laid up for three months, and he lost his job at MGM. After that Kilroy had quit the rodeos for good and taken a job with United Artists Records in Nashville. In the fall of 1967, when he was twenty-six, he left United Artists and joined Mercury.

"Jerry Lee and I had been friends forever, it seemed. The first place I ever saw him was at the Wagon Wheel in Natchez. I had been rodeoin' since I was twelve, and I rodeo'd all over Louisiana. If Jerry Lee was workin' anywhere near where I was travelin', I'd go see him. We'd drink together, fool around. Then, in 1958, his cousin Mickey Gilley and I put a band together. Played Ray's Lounge in Lake Charles, Louisiana. I married a girl there, and Mickey was best man at my wedding. When my wife and I split up, I moved in with Mickey down in Houston. We sold used cars together, worked for his brother-in-law."

When Kilroy came to Mercury, he met with Charlie Fach, the boss of the New York office, and Fach asked him what he intended to do to create some excitement down in Nashville.

"Let's put Jerry Lee country," Kilroy said.

"Oh, Jesus, shit, no, Eddie," Fach sputtered. "He's got less than a year to run on his contract. Kennedy doesn't wanna mess with him. Nobody wants to mess with him. Jerry Lee's unhappy with us, we're unhappy with him. We're just going to let the whole thing disappear."

"No," Kilroy said. "That's wrong. He can be a smash country act."

"Oh, shit, Eddie, he won't record anymore."

"Well, if he will, can we do a project?"

"Yeah," said Fach, "I guess so, but we're really not interested in him, we're really not."

Kilroy got on the telephone and tracked down Jerry Lee, who was in Ferriday.

"What're you doin', Killer?" Eddie said to him.

"Aw, nothin'," said Jerry Lee. "Me and Cecil are fishin'."

"Well, I just started workin' for Mercury 'bout two weeks ago."

"Well, that's funny as hell, 'cause I'm fixin' t'leave them sonofabitches. They ain't worth fuckin' shit."

"Let me cut a country session on ya."

"Well, I'll think about it. Me and Cecil, we'll talk about it."

Three days later, Cecil telephoned Eddie Kilroy and told him that Jerry Lee was willing to cut for Smash one more time, but only as a favor to an old friend.

"I had to go out on the road that afternoon to make a bunch of distributors," Kilroy recalled. "Before I left I called every credible publisher in town and asked for material for Jerry Lee. I got back to town two weeks later, the same day that he was gonna arrive. I drove straight to my office, and there were three acetates on my desk. That was all the material that had come in. Nobody wanted a Jerry Lee Lewis cut. I thought, Holy God, this is embarrassing.

"I went home, and Jerry Lee called. I went by his hotel to pick him up. We stopped at the liquor store on Division Street, got us a fifth, went up to my office. I didn't wanna tell him that nobody wanted a Jerry Lee record, so I went into this story about how my secretary had fucked up, this and that. And those three acetates weren't any good, we both knew that. So Jerry Lee started in: 'Hell, what the fuck, we'll cut "Your Cheatin' Heart." ' I said, 'No, no, that ain't it.'

"Well, I knew this song that Del Reeves had cut when I was at United Artists. It was a ballad, and Del Reeves couldn't come off with a ballad. I knew U.A. wasn't gonna release it. It

was a hell of a song, written by Jerry Chesnut. So, about midnight that night I called up Chesnut and told him, 'If you
bring me a dub of "Another Place, Another Time," I'll cut it
on Jerry Lee tomorrow.' A few minutes later, Chesnut drove
up in his pajamas, blew his horn, and handed me the acetate. I
played it for Jerry Lee, and he thought it was pretty damn
good. We went into the studio the next day and cut it. I didn't
get any credit for producin' the record, 'cause Jerry Kennedy
had a contract that said he had to produce everything that was
cut for Mercury in Nashville. I bailed out of the company
about six months later."

"Another Place, Another Time" was a beautiful song of anguish and loneliness, and Jerry Lee sang it in the studio that
cold, gray afternoon, January 9, 1968, with the voice of one
trying to conceal rather than to reveal that anguish and that
loneliness. It was a voice as strong and as enduring and as solitary as his daddy's grin, and like that grin it seemed to contain
all the sadness in the world; and when Eddie Kilroy and the
musicians who were in the studio that day heard that voice,
they felt shivers like cold crawling things up and down their
spines, and they closed and opened their eyes, breathing, as if
to shake loose a sudden inward fright.

> One by one they're turning out the lights.
> I been feedin' that old jukebox just to hold you tight.
> Yes, it's for the best I just put in my last dime,
> Heard you whisper we'd meet again, another place, another
>   time.
>
> Chairs are stacked on the tables and it's closing time they
>   say.
> I could wait right here forever if they'd only let me stay.
> Anywhere would be much better than that old lonely room of
>   mine

And a sleepless night a-waiting for another place, another
   time.

Won't that room of mine be a lonely place to be
After I been holdin' you so close to me,
And won't that old stairway be a little hard to climb
To a lonely room to wait for another place, another time.
Won't that old stairway be a little hard to climb
To a lonely room to wait for another place, another time.

The record hit the country charts in the first week of March,
and it rose, and it kept rising, till it was a Top Ten country
hit. It stayed on the country charts for more than four months,
and it crossed over to the pop charts. For the first time in ten
long years, Jerry Lee Lewis's voice was heard throughout the
South. It was a different voice—older, tougher, darker, and
shorn of all innocence. But it was his voice, and he was alive.
He cast to the ground whiskey and he cast to the ground pills,
the entwined, killing serpents of his many-yeared succor; and
with the clear, cutting eyes of the hawk he watched that returned whore, errant fame, raise her skirt, and he felt her belly
warm to his, and he threw back his head and he roared as he
had never roared before.

The whore brought new, unexpected gifts. On the evening
of March 5, as "Another Place, Another Time" was beginning
to be heard throughout the South, Jerry Lee walked onto the
stage of the Ahmanson Theatre in Los Angeles. He wore a fur-
trimmed jerkin and a necklace of large, tear-shaped jewels,
and he told the audience that he was not Iago of Venice, but
rather Jerry Lee Lewis, the old honky-tonk nighttime man
from down yonder, removed to this strange time and place,
neither then nor now, here nor there; and he strode to a great
green-and-gold piano, and he narrowed his eyes and raked the
keys.

Jack Good, the man who had brought Jerry Lee to "Shindig" in 1964, had wanted to direct a rock-'n'-roll version of *Othello* since the fifties, when he had been president of the Oxford University Drama Society. In 1958, during Jerry Lee's ruinous British tour, Good had observed him stalking in anger across the lobby of the Westbury Hotel, and he immediately decided that Jerry Lee would one day play the role of Iago in his dreamed-of production. As the years passed, Good's involvements, first with the Beatles, then with "Shindig," had stood in the way of his bringing a rock-'n'-roll *Othello* to the stage. By the summer of 1965, after leaving "Shindig," he had hired Ray Pohlman, the musical director of "Shindig," to compose some songs that would fit well into various scenes of Shakespeare's play. Within a year, the score, nineteen songs in all, was completed and Good began casting for the production, which he now called *Catch My Soul,* from a phrase uttered by Othello in Act III. *The New York Times* of August 22, 1966, announced that Jerry Lee had been signed by Good to appear as Iago, and that Rosie Grier, the Los Angeles Rams tackle, had been signed to play the Moor Othello. The show was scheduled to open that fall at the Shubert Theatre on Broadway. The opening was later postponed until March, 1967, then at last rescheduled to open not in New York but in Los Angeles, as the fourth and final production of the Center Theater Group's 1968 season. Rosie Grier was replaced by Peter Brock, and Brock was eventually replaced by William Marshall, who had played the role of Othello in more conventional productions. (Rosie Grier was to receive a certain notoriety as an actor four years later, when, in his movie debut, he co-starred with Ray Milland as half of *The Thing with Two Heads.*)

The cast rehearsals began on the morning of January 22, less than two weeks after Jerry Lee recorded "Another Place, Another Time." Jack Good and the rest of the crew were sur-

'T was mine, 't is his, and has been slave to thousands;
But he that filches from me my good name,
Robs me of that which not enriches him,
And makes me poor indeed.

Catch My Soul closed on April 13, after grossing more than $500,000. Six days later Jerry Lee was in Nashville, recording again. Of the eight songs he cut at this session, "What's Made Milwaukee Famous (Has Made a Loser Out of Me)," a hard-edged barroom lament written for him by Nashville songwriter Glenn Sutton, was chosen to be his next single. The record was released on May 13, and a week later Smash issued an album, *Another Place, Another Time,* that included both the hit record of that title and the new single. "What's Made Milwaukee Famous" broke into the country charts during the first week of June. It remained on the charts for four months, rising higher than "Another Place, Another Time" had risen, clear to the Number Two position, and crossing over to the pop charts in July. By summer's end, the single had sold more than 170,000 copies, and the album more than 85,000.

On June 26 he made his first network TV appearance in almost three years, on "The Joey Bishop Show," singing "Great Balls of Fire," "Another Place, Another Time," and closing with one of Iago's demonic soliloquies. After a tour of the Southwest, he left on July 20 for a three-week tour of England, where, on August 9, his performance at the Sunbury Jazz & Blues Festival drove the sedate audience to a state of Holy Ghost frenzy, then to one of riot, a state of riot so pure and wild and frightening that festival officials, fearing mass violence, forced Jerry Lee to cease his hands and his mouth and to depart the stage. Five days later, he was back in Nashville recording more country songs. One of these, "She Still Comes

Around (To Love What's Left of Me)," a new song written for him by Glenn Sutton, was released as a single in September, and it became Jerry Lee's second Number Two country hit in a row.

September marked the end of Jerry Lee's fifth year with Smash, and he signed a new, very lucrative three-year contract with the label. (At this time his sister Linda Gail was also given a contract to record for Smash.) On November 12, after returning from a three-week tour of Germany, Jerry Lee recorded a new song called "To Make Love Sweeter for You," written by Glenn Sutton and Jerry Kennedy. The record was released a short time before Christmas, and a few weeks later Jerry Lee had his first Number One hit since "Great Balls of Fire."

As 1969 began, Jerry Lee was the hottest country singer in the South. He did not forsake the rock-'n'-roll people, the younger kin of those who had shook and sweated to his unholy howlings more than a decade before. On Friday, the thirteenth of December, he had appeared at the L.A. Forum with the Doors, with Jim Morrison, younger than he, but doomed as he from the womb to destruction. On April 14, 1969, as a favor to Jack Good, he appeared on the Monkees' NBC-TV special, "33⅓ Revolutions Per Monkee," singing "Whole Lotta Shakin' Goin' On" and "Down the Line." But he knew that it was the country people, the older sunburnt, woods-eyed people of his own blood, who were now putting the gold in his pocket, and he gave them what they desired, and he gave it to them good, singing his country songs raw and pure and hard, as few had since the days of Hank Williams and Lefty Frizzell. Before the year was out, Jerry Lee had followed "To Make Love Sweeter For You" with two more Top Ten country hits, "She Even Woke Me Up to Say Goodbye" and "Once More with Feeling"; and all three of his 1969 albums were so successful that they crossed over to the pop LP charts. He was making more money than he ever had in his life.

And he had done something he had not intended to do. He had stirred Elvis from seclusion. Since 1965 there had been no Top Ten pop singles for Elvis, no Top Ten country singles. Fewer and fewer people were buying his albums or paying to see his movies. In the summer of 1968, when Jerry Lee's voice had once again, after years in the desert, come to be heard throughout the South, Elvis had gone into the NBC studio in Burbank and taped a TV special. (In one part of the show, he was backed by the Blossoms, the former "Shindig" vocal group that had backed Jerry Lee in *Catch My Soul*.) Broadcast on December 3, the one-hour special, "Elvis," effectively revived both his career and his confidence. In July, 1969, he performed in concert for the first time in almost eight years, at the International Hotel in Las Vegas, bringing an end to his retreat from the public and renewing in Jerry Lee's heart the desire to wrest the throne of that kingdom that now, in 1969, no longer was but behind the uncalm eyes of these two unusual thirty-four-year-old men who lived in opposite parts of Memphis, Tennessee.

Jerry Lee lifted to him again the entwined serpents of his succor, and he howled. On October 15, three weeks after taping a series of five half-hour TV specials at the Holiday Inn Dinner Theatre in Memphis, Jerry Lee traveled to Nashville to attend the eighteenth annual D.J. Convention. On the night of his arrival, he appeared as a guest performer at the nationally televised Country Music Awards show, held at the Ryman Auditorium. He wore a dark, vested, pinstripe suit, regimental-stripe tie, and white sneakers. After the various awards were presented, ending with Johnny Cash's award for Entertainer of the Year, Jerry Lee was heard to say that "None of them cats could've followed me on stage. They could all go out there on stage nekkid and I could still take 'em beatin' on the piano with m'damn foot! Hell, man, I think *I* shoulda won Entertainer of the Year!"

A few days later, on October 20, as the D.J. Convention was winding down, Jerry Lee cut eight songs at the Monument Studio. One of these songs, "Once More with Feeling," written for him over several bottles of wine the day before by Kris Kristofferson and Shel Silverstein, would become his next hit single. After the session, Jerry Lee sat in the studio, drinking Scotch throughout the night, playing the tape of "Once More with Feeling" over and over, and talking out of the side of his mouth to a Pentagon barber, the barber's wife, and *Rolling Stone* reporter John Grissim. By one o'clock in the afternoon, the Scotch was finished, and Jerry Lee and John Grissim drove to the Continental Hotel, where Jerry Lee was staying. The reporter switched on his cassette recorder as Jerry Lee swaggered down the hall, yelling at a handful of motel maids who were sorting laundry in an alcove.

"Get outa heah!" he roared, then swaggered on, unlocking the door to his room. "Yeah, jes' move 'em all outa the damn way. I've killed more people for less than that. I'm a vi'lent mothahumper today. Don't nobody, don't nobody fool with me, or I'll kill!" He fell down on the bed. "Yessir, do this all the time. Strength unlimited. Hell, that's a hell of a damn title, Strength Unlimited, Inc." He laughed, then he ceased laughing. "Hell, I smoke pot. Pills, dope, needle, Ex-Lax. I drink whiskey, Scotch, gin, vodka, piss, vinegar—whadaya think of that!" He closed his eyes, then he opened them. "Snuff queens? Hell, where they at? I'd like t'meet 'em. They done all faded out." He laughed again, then he stopped laughing again. "Naw, I ain't lookin' for no broad. I don't need no broad. I don't need no pills. I don't need nothin'. Few good drinks an' I'm all right."

Cecil Harrelson entered the room and asked Jerry Lee where in the hell he had disappeared to, told him that he had been worried about him.

"Cecil," Jerry Lee said, grinning, "I called all three of my wives. Yup, straight across the board. Even Dorothy. She's crazy but she loves me. They all love me." Then he started singing "Once More with Feeling," picking up the phone to call room service as Cecil and the *Rolling Stone* reporter began to converse, Cecil telling the reporter than Jerry Lee had never disappeared like this before.

"Honey," Jerry Lee was saying into the receiver, "is that all I end up with, a sandwich? I been up all day an' all night roarin'. Yeah, I may be an idiot, but I'm tryin' t'settle down. I don't care what you look like, but I love ya. You can do it, mama. Yessir, give it all you got. That's right, baby. I'm talkin' to the sweetest thing in the world. I wanna tell her to"—he started singing—"'Try it one more time with feelin', darlin', take it from the top.' All right, baby, what're we gonna do? When do you git off? Well, come on up. Might be pretty good. I love ya, I love ya. Well, hell, a club sandwich an' two large glasses of milk. With a cherry in 'em, 'cause they're hard t'find. Huh? Well, I ain't lookin' for one. Naw, I want you. Naw, I didn't mean that t'be insultin', I'm jes' jokin'. Well, thank ya, baby," he said, and hung up the phone. Cecil suggested to Jerry Lee that he try to get some sleep.

"This body ain't weary," Jerry Lee said. "I ain't ready to go to bed. *I'm jes' gettin' warmed up!* I'll eat m'sandwich, and you git me a couple more drinks, and I'll go again. I'll be up for another night, run clear through the whole building. *Arrgh!*"

In this manner, Jerry Lee Lewis entered his thirty-fifth year.

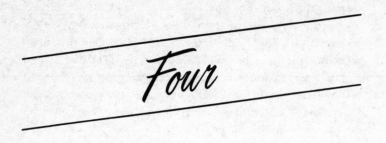

Four

Jimmy Lee Swaggart had come a long way from street preaching. Since 1960 he had recorded seven albums of gospel music. (The second of these albums, *God Took Away My Yesterdays*, had been cut, with the help of Jerry Lee, at the Sun studio in Memphis in 1962.) He had built a house in Baton Rouge in 1967, using it as the headquarters of his evangelical crusade. On January 1, 1969, he had begun his syndicated radio ministry, "The Camp Meeting Hour"—"I want you on the radio," the Lord had told him—and it was growing steadily. Later that same year, he became the youngest evangelist ever to preach at the General Council of the Assemblies of God. The folks back in Ferriday were proud of Jimmy Lee, as they were of Jerry Lee, but many of his kin were riled at the way he was beginning to speak of them in his sermons.

In the summer of 1968, when Jerry Lee's second fame had begun to flower full, Lee Calhoun had been stricken with chill darkness and he had almost died. Jimmy Lee was preaching at the time at the Assembly Tabernacle in Atlanta, and his younger sister Jeanette called him to say that Uncle Lee was dying. A year later he stood before hundreds of Christians at the Oak Cliff Assembly of God Church in Dallas. He preached a sermon in which he told that Uncle Lee, whom he called a "vile, vulgar, profane old man," had during his close call with death seen a vision of hell so real that he had imagined his feet to be aflame in the Inferno.

On November 14, 1969, not long after Jimmy Lee Swaggart had stood and preached his sermon about Uncle Lee, the astronaut Charles Conrad, Jr., carried to the moon with him aboard Apollo 12 a ninety-minute Highlander cassette of Jerry Lee Lewis music. Mamie told Uncle Lee about this, and he smiled and shook his head in quiet, confounded laughter. He had come from another century. There had not even been such things as gasoline cars when he was a boy. Now his nephew, whom he had heard strike those first wild notes a quarter of a century ago in his, Lee Calhoun's, own parlor; his nephew, who bore his name and many of his ways; his nephew was being heard on the moon. When he was little, he and his daddy would frog-hunt at night along the Cocodrie, and his daddy would tell him all about the moon, how it was a million miles away, and how there were queer little critters, sort of like Chinee, living on it, and how it was made out of mother-of-pearl. Even as a little boy, he did not believe any of this; but he had liked the pitch-black night and the sound of his daddy's voice, warming him. That was in that other century.

A week or so later, Uncle Lee summoned his wife, Stella, and her sister Mamie, and he had them lift him from his wheelchair and carry him to the bank. He would not be seen in that contraption in public. He went into the vault with the president of the bank, and they stayed in there for a good hour.

Then he had Stella and Mamie carry him home again. For days after this, he said very little.

He was stricken again with the chill darkness and taken to the Concordia Parish Hospital. There, on the cold night of December 16, he died, screaming nothing of the fire or the flames.

Two mornings later, at the Church of God on Mississippi Avenue, the preacher stood over his coffin and spoke of great men and their rewards. Then the coffin was taken to the little cemetery near Clayton, where the pallbearers—his brothers, brothers-in-law, and his favorite nephew, Jerry Lee—carried him to his space in the dirt and threw flowers down upon him. As Jerry Lee turned away to leave, an old man came up close to him and took him by the arm.

"Son," he said, "I'll tell you something, you piano-pluckin' bastard. If you had only listened to old Calhoun."

That was all the old man said. Then he got into a 1962 Chevy, and he drove away. Jerry Lee stared at the back end of the car as it moved slowly down the road. The old man was H. L. Hunt.

"The richest man in the world drivin' a '62 Chevrolet," Jerry Lee recalled years later. "And he didn't even have any of my records in it. Judge not lest you be judged; but that old bastard went to hell. You can believe that."

Five

The hit records continued to come for Jerry Lee throughout 1970, and his concert price eventually rose to $10,000 a night. He bought his own plane, a DC-3, and he hired a pilot. In May he flew with his band and his kin to Las Vegas, where he recorded a live album at the International Hotel, the same hotel that Elvis had appeared at the year before. Jerry Lee's son, Jerry Lee, Jr., who was now fifteen, had left his mother, Jane, and begun traveling with his father. He stood onstage at the International, among the band, and he beat a tambourine. Later he told his daddy that he wanted to be a drummer, that his daddy could have two drummers in his band.

"Jerry came to me one week," recalled Tarp Tarrant, who was still drumming behind him. "This was in September, 1970. We had a show coming up at the Coliseum. It was about eight days away. He said, 'I want you to take Junior out to your house in the country. I want you to teach him to play like you.' So I took Junior out there to my house. Stayed out there a week or so. And I found out then, when we got there, that Junior was doin' dope. He was takin' pills and smokin' grass, drinkin' beer like it was goin' out of style. I encouraged him to leave it alone, 'cause I could see that he couldn't handle it. He was so young and he'd gotten himself so strung out. But I taught him how to play drums, and we took him on the road with us. When Jerry eventually discovered that Junior was strung out, he started accusin' me of bein' the one who got him started. He cussed me out and told me that he knew it for a fact but that he couldn't prove it. He said, 'If I could prove it, I'd kill ya.' There were several times on the plane, man, I'd wake up—y'know, like, after a show we'd get on the plane, I'd take a handful of Placidyl and drink a couple beers and then kick back—I'd wake up with a knife right here, man—right at the bottom of my throat. I said, 'Hey, man, you got the holdin' hand—do whatever you're gonna do.'

"See, Jerry was gettin' farther and farther out. We'd get back to Memphis after a long haul, he'd say, 'The first one of you motherfuckin' bastards that leave is fired. We're gonna party for five fuckin' days.' He'd yell to Cecil, 'Don't pay nobody. Everybody's supposed to meet in my office. Anyone's not there he's fired and he don't get his money.' That was a trip, man. We had to go through all that shit. We'd go there, stay two or three days, not wantin' to be there. Me wantin' to be home with my family. I'd have my wife come to the airport to pick me up many times, then I'd send her home, get in the car with him and leave. Because I wanted to try and get my money. If I went home and came back to try to get it, I might get my brains blowed out or get beat up or something. That was the kind of scene that was going on."

Not long after Jerry Lee's thirty-fifth birthday, Myra Gale

and he decided that it would be financially wise to make her the legal owner of their home at 5042 East Shore Drive. On October 21, they signed a document that rendered Myra Gale the landlord and Jerry Lee the tenant of their home, with the permanent title to the property going to the party who should live longer. After this, Jerry Lee departed for a tour of Australia.

Myra Gale had hired the two detectives the previous spring. The detectives, Peter Malito and Richard Bierer of Accredited Security Systems, had been gathering evidence of Jerry Lee's sins.

On November 9, while Jerry Lee was in Australia, Myra Gale filed a divorce suit against him. Her bill of complaint accused Jerry Lee of various infidelities, beginning with the summer of their remarriage, when, she claimed, Jerry Lee had returned from a California trip and told Myra that he was in love with another girl. Her bill stated that since 1964 "complainant has been subject to every type of physical and mental abuse imaginable." She said that Jerry Lee threatened to "hire people to throw complainant in the river and to throw acid in her face." She said that in 1960 Jerry Lee jerked a cigarette from her mouth, threatened to stick it in her eye, and finally put it out against the flesh of her arm. And, she said, he "drinks constantly."

Shelby County Deputies served Jerry Lee with the divorce papers as he stepped from a plane a few days later. He stared at what the papers said, and he shook his head and sadly swore.

He went home, where Myra was not. He drank and he closed his eyes and he must have pictured the way her clove-brown hair had curled at her ear that evening long ago as they flew from England; and he drank.

On November 25, the day before Thanksgiving, Jerry Lee

was sitting alone in the house on East Shore Drive. He decided that he had gone as far as he could go and that it was time to straighten out his life. He called the pastor at the Church of God, and then he called Cecil Harrelson. And then he drove south to Ferriday.

Two weeks later, on December 10, Cecil announced to the press that Jerry Lee would no longer perform at nightclubs. The reason for this, he stated, was that liquor was served at such places.

The following afternoon, Jack Hurst, a staff correspondent for the Nashville *Tennessean,* interviewed Jerry Lee in Memphis, at the office of National Artists Attractions, the company that booked most of Jerry Lee's shows. Hurst asked him about the divorce.

"I'm a fair man and I've taken care of a lot of people," Jerry Lee told him. "I've been good to my wife and my mother and my father and my sisters and my children. Matter of fact, I've given them my life. I've given them everything I've made. And I really don't think I deserve to be treated exactly the way I'm being treated right now by my wife. I'm a little bitter about that."

Then Hurst asked him about his return to the church and about his decision to quit the nightclubs.

"I've made a stand for God," Jerry Lee said. "I'm just letting the people know openly that I went back to the church and I got myself saved, and the Lord forgave me of my sins and wiped 'em away.

"I think if my fans, the people that follow me and like me, got a good, clean, God-fearing Jerry Lee Lewis, they'd like him better.

"From here on in, I'm only gonna play at coliseums and fairs, and I'm gonna have about fifteen minutes of gospel music at the end of each show, and I'll give my testimony.

"I don't know exactly how I'm gonna handle it. Mostly, there'll be no drinkin' and cursin' and carryin' on. Wild parties and all this kinda stuff.

"I believe God will give me wisdom enough to make this decision. I'll just pray and see what happens."

THE SECRET PARTS OF THE NIGHT

On the day after Easter, in 1971, Mamie Lewis slipped into darkness and was taken to the Concordia Parish Hospital. She died there the following week, at the stroke of midnight, April 21. Jerry Lee brought her body back to the home he had bought for her. Midnight came again, and Jerry Lee called Earl LeBouef, owner of the LeBouef Studio & Camera Center in Natchez; called him at his home and told him to come across the river to Ferriday, to take pictures of his mother's body; and this was done. When day broke, her body was taken to the Church of God, then to the little cemetery near Clayton.

In October, 1969, Jerry Lee had recorded a song called "In Loving Memories," written by his manager, Cecil, and his sister, Linda Gail. It was a sad song about the funeral of a loved one. Mamie Lewis had been with Jerry Lee at the session that day, and he had called her into the studio to sing harmony behind him, along with Linda Gail. The record became a modest country hit in February and March, 1971. Now, on this April day, he told the man what to chisel on Mamie's tombstone.

A MOTHER WHO WAS THE SUNSHINE OF OUR WORLD WILL REMAIN IN OUR LOVING MEMORIES

"After Mother's death, something changed inside him," Frankie Jean said. "He could not cope with it. He didn't even want to come and see Mama when she was sick. He came very few times. He just could not cope with it. He could not stand it. He never wanted to see his mother die. Linda Gail wound up in a hospital for twelve months. She had to quit working for Jerry. She was really sick, lost down to ninety-eight pounds. I don't think it was her mind. I think she lost the will to live. And where can you put a person that's lost the will to live? You put them in a hospital and get them well. You have to have a psychiatrist to help you. She would've never made it without Dr. Sexton. He's in Memphis."

In the first, dark hours of April 23, the day after Jerry Lee laid his mother to rest, a cruel windstorm swept through Memphis. Jerry Lee's Douglas DC-3 was parked and moored at Hi-Air, a private airport on Democrat Road. The Hecate wind took that DC-3 and hurled it across the ramp, smashing it against a parked Cessna. Jerry Lee went out and bought him a bigger plane, a better plane, a Convair 640 turbojet with twenty-six seats and a bar. It cost him $160,000 with a trade-in allowance for the Hecate-wrecked DC-3.

Three weeks later, on May 12, the divorce became final. Judge Howard Brugge awarded Myra Gale the house on East Shore Drive, $175,000 (tax-free), two Mark III Lincoln Continentals, and sole custody of their seven-year-old daughter,

Jerry Lee and Elmo, skyborne, 1972.

Phoebe. Myra allowed Jerry Lee to remain at the house, for she had moved into a new home, at 847 Candace.

On September 3, four months after the divorce, Myra Gale married Peter Malito, the private detective she had hired to investigate her husband. They were married at the home of her parents, JW and Lois Brown. Little Phoebe served as flower girl.

A month later, on October 1, Jerry Lee was sued by a woman, Mrs. Ann McMahon, who claimed that he had verbally and physically assaulted her during his recent performance at the El Capitan South Supper Club in Memphis. She complained that he had insulted her, that he had directed these insults into a microphone, that he had thrown a hardbound book at her, twisted her arm, and tried to drag her across the electric organ he was playing. He denied all charges.

On the following Thursday, October 7, Jerry Lee married a twenty-nine-year-old Memphis divorcée named Jaren Elizabeth Gunn Pate. They separated two weeks later.

On January 14, 1972, Jerry Lee strode into the Mercury Studio in Nashville. He poured him a drink, looked around, and nodded in imperious approval. Crowded into the studio were ten musicians, six background vocalists, and a seventeen-piece orchestra.

"He wanted everybody there," Jerry Kennedy recalled. "He didn't want anything overdubbed later. It was a mess. We had an acre of people there—voices, strings, everything. And, as always, Jerry Lee started changin' keys, and the arranger was goin' crazy, havin' to rewrite stuff for the string section, 'cause they just could not change keys like that; they needed charts. We only cut three songs that day. One of 'em was 'Chantilly Lace,' the old Big Bopper thing from the fifties."

Hello! you good-lookin' thing, you!

After howling this greeting into the microphone, Jerry Lee breathed, audibly, lasciviously, as he had not done on a record in almost fifteen years. Then he lowered his voice, and he said:

> *Yeah—huh?*
> *Now, this is the Killer speakin'—*
> *Do I like what?*
> *I sure do like it, baby.*

His fingers came down upon the keyboard then, and he pounded those keys as only he could, and he began to sing "Chantilly Lace," sing it with the fiery surliness that had been his and his alone back in the fifties and was, he now knew, his alone still. After almost three minutes, he was lost in the song, howling, burning, pounding, changing keys and meters. The orchestra could not follow him. Suddenly, Jerry Lee heard the voice of the arranger saying something about "sixteen bars," telling the orchestra not to worry, "we'll get it right next time."

"I can hear that back there," Jerry Lee yelled. "Sonofabitch is talkin' on my goddamn record. To hell with it! I'm still hangin' it in like Gunga Din! *Yeow!*" He recommenced pounding and howling.

Jerry Kennedy cut the final minutes from the recording, fading it after two minutes and fifty seconds. Mercury (since 1970 the company had stopped using the Smash imprint) released the record six weeks later. On March 4 it hit the pop charts; then, a week later, it hit the country charts. Before it had run its course, "Chantilly Lace" rose to Number One on the country charts and Number 43 on the pop charts. (It also made its way to Number 23 on the Easy Listening charts.) *The "Killer" Rocks On,* the album that included the single, sold more copies than any album he had ever made.

On April 21 Jerry Lee departed for a long tour of Europe. His wife, Jaren, with whom he had reconciled, entered Baptist Hospital in Memphis that same day, suffering from pregnancy complications. Six days later, on April 27, she gave birth to a daughter, and she named her Lori Leigh Lewis.

Jerry Lee returned to Memphis only to discover that Myra Gale, who had moved with her new husband to Stone Mountain, Georgia, was suing him for $19,700 in back alimony. He was ordered to appear in court on August 3, but instead he flew to London, where he was to perform at Wembley Stadium on the fifth. His lawyer stood before Circuit Court Judge Brugge and explained that the check was in the mail.

"Mr. Lewis has the keys to the jail in his pocket," the judge warned. "I don't want him back here troubling the court again."

At the end of 1972 Jerry Lee formed his own company, Jerry Lee Lewis Enterprises, Inc., located in a suite of offices at 3003 Airways Boulevard in Memphis. In addition to his manager, Cecil Harrelson (who was now married to Linda Gail), Jerry Lee hired Roy Dean as his booking agent and Eddie Kilroy as his creative director.

On January 6, 1973, Jerry Lee, Cecil, Kilroy, Ken Lovelace, Jerry Lee, Jr., and Judd Phillips (who had now resurfaced as Jerry Lee's advisor and drinking partner) arrived in London for four days of sessions at Advision Studios. Mercury's idea was to have Jerry Lee cut an album with various British rock stars: Alvin Lee, Tony Ashton, Peter Frampton, Rory Gallagher, Chas Hodges, and others. The album that resulted from this week in London, a two-record set called *The Session,* was released in March. It rose to the Top Forty on both the pop and country LP charts, and a single from the album, a loud, drunken version of "Drinkin' Wine, Spo-Dee-O-Dee," the song he had driven that crowd in the Ford lot wild with back in 1949, rose to Number 41 on the pop charts and Number 20 on the country charts.

But there was something eerie about that week in London, at least as far as Eddie Kilroy was concerned. Jerry Lee, Jr., had been behaving strangely, and on this trip he had been entrusted to Kilroy, who shared a room with him at the Royal Lancaster Hotel near Hyde Park.

"Junior kept pacin' the floor," Kilroy recalled. "He walked back and forth imitatin' his daddy. 'I'm the Killer! I'm the Killer! I'm the great Jerry Lee Lewis!' One night he took about ten or twelve baths, said he couldn't sleep. He told me that he thought a little boy and a little girl from Ferriday were livin' in his belly. He said he felt 'em, and that they were troubled. It was a hard thing to take—only eighteen years old and already gone."

Back home, Eddie Kilroy arranged for Jerry Lee to make his debut on "The Grand Ole Opry." "They didn't wanna let him on," Eddie said. "I had to promise them that he wouldn't cuss, that he wouldn't show up drunk, that he'd do only country songs. So he shows up that night, goes onstage, and completely fucks with their heads. There was Ernest Tubb, Hank Snow, Roy Acuff, lookin' around the curtains at this wildman out there."

Jerry Lee did not say a word as he sat down at the piano that night of January 20. He went right into "Another Place, Another Time," the song that had brought him back five years before. Then, with barely a pause, he began pounding out a manic version of "What'd I Say." For almost a half hour, he alternated country songs with rock 'n' roll, refusing to stop for the scheduled commercial breaks. He called out Del Wood, the woman who had befriended him on his 1954 journey to

Nashville, and they sat at the piano together, pounding out her old hit, "Down Yonder." By then the crowd was in the palm of his hand, wild, as no other Opry crowd had been since Hank Williams's debut in 1949. He tore into Chuck Berry's "Johnny B. Goode," then "Great Balls of Fire," then "Whole Lotta Shakin' Goin' On."

"Y'know somethin', neighbors," he said, his hands still pounding the Holy Ghost rhythm of his first, great hit, "this song, 'Whole Lotta Shakin' Goin' On,' was a Number One country-and-Western tune, Number One rock-'n'-roll tune, Number One rhythm-'n'-blues tune. It makes no difference really. You are what you are. You can do what you can do. And I thank God that Jerry Lee Lewis can do it!"

The crowd roared and stomped and whistled, and when they did this, Jerry Lee began to sing Merle Haggard's "Workin' Man Blues," and when the crowd recommenced roaring and stomping and whistling, he stopped singing that song in mid-line, and he went into "Rock Around the Clock," then back into "Whole Lotta Shakin' Goin' On." He stood and howled "Chantilly Lace," playing the piano with the heel of his boot; and then he waited for the crowd to cease their noise of frenzy, and he beheld them.

"Let me tell ya somethin' about Jerry Lee Lewis, ladies and gentlemen," he said. "I am a rock-'n'-rollin', country-and-Western, rhythm-'n'-blues-singin' mothafucker."

Disregarding the distraught gestures of the "Opry" managers at stage left, he descended upon the piano and began to sing "Good Golly, Miss Molly." Then, abruptly, he fell still, closed his eyes, and performed the most perfectly sad rendition of Hank Williams's "I'm So Lonesome I Could Cry" that anyone had ever heard; and he left the stage and flew home to Memphis.

That spring he bought a second plane, a Cessna 340, and a

new home, a thirty-acre ranch located in Nesbit, Mississippi, a few miles from Hernando, where he and Myra Gale had been married fifteen years before. The Nesbit house, situated on the west side of Malone Road, had been built in 1966 by the president of a Memphis construction company, and it contained six bedrooms, six bathrooms, three living rooms, a kitchen, a dining room, and a den. The price of the ranch, which also included a five-acre lake, was $190,000. Here Jerry Lee and Elmo, sometimes their women, always the shades of those who came before, lived.

"He ended up throwin' everything away," said Eddie Kilroy, remembering that spring of 1973. "He didn't save a nickel. Nothing was being run as a business. We had a lot of money, but he refused to pay his Gulf Oil bills. They took our credit cards. Consequently, the only way that we could get gas to fuel the plane was to pay cash. We found ourselves walkin' around with $50,000 or $60,000 in a briefcase. No records kept. It was really bizarre. At one time he probably had eighteen or twenty people on the payroll, not countin' the relatives he would carry from time to time.

"He began to get very heavy into the roarin' scene—worse than before. He started blowin' dates, fuckin' up sessions. I guess the money fell away. I quit around then, the middle of '73."

The country hits became smaller and smaller, and none of them crossed to the pop charts. The $10,000 bookings became fewer and fewer. And the night began to wear the scent of sulphur.

"A man ain't got but two choices, heaven or hell," he heard himself saying. It was not his voice, perhaps. Yes, that was it. He opened his eyes and saw who he was talking to. For almost

225

twenty years now, he had been in a different bar in a different city every night. He had met a lot of these people. They drank with him, and then they had something to talk about for six months or a year or whatever, until the next time they ran into him. They were a bunch of fucking idiots, and this was one of them.

"Heaven or hell," he heard himself repeating. "A man's got a soul, he ain't no animal. A man's got a soul, and that soul ain't goin' but one of two places, heaven or hell. I know that, but I can't seem to . . . I don't know what's wrong with me. God said, 'I am the alpho and the omego, the beginnin' an' the end.' The rich man ask Abraham to send Lazarus, 'Dip thy finger in the pool and cool these parched lips.'

"God gave me a talent, an *unlimited* talent. I got to be right or it wouldn't plague me day an' night. What am I searchin' for? *Happiness?*"

"You're searchin' for help," the fucking idiot said.

"What is happiness?"

"It's within yourself."

"I ain't found any of it, man. I know what it is to go in there, lay down on the bed, close your eyes, and know everything ain't right."

"You been there."

"So you drink. So you pop a pill. So you rock. You search, you try to satisfy yourself. I know the story, I been there."

"You been there."

Jerry Lee heard a woman's voice saying, "We have to go on in just a moment." He looked around. He was backstage. Bachelors III, yes, that was it—Fort Lauderdale. He emptied his glass, then filled it.

"I lost my wife," he said. "This"—he snapped his fingers—"brought some things to my attention. But I can't seem to . . . Jimmy Lee Swaggart's done it. That's what makes me mad. We learned to play on the same piano. Ran into him the other day. Boy, he got on me hot and heavy. That man is a powerhouse for God. We both were at one time. But you can't serve two masters, for ya'll end up hatin' one and lovin' the other. 'Be ye hot or cold, for if ye be lukewarm I'll spew ya outa My mouth.' You're goin' to heaven or you're goin' to hell. There's no in-between.

"Well, I'm in a great mood now."

Linda Gail entered the room and chirped to Jerry Lee.

"What make a man drink?" he asked. "What make a man make a *fool* outa hisself? *He's a weaklin'!* Oh, you can hit somebody, poke 'im, arm-wrassle 'im, all that stuff. You still weak as water. To be a real strong man—*hah!* There's a horse of a differ'nt color. To *walk out that door* and do what you're *s'posed* to do."

"I can't drink," said Linda Gail, giggling.

"Well, *I* can drink," he said, turning to his sister. The fucking idiot seemed to have vanished. Maybe he had not been there to start with. Fuck him. "I can drink. That's great, isn't it? That really makes me great. Jerry Lee Lewis can handle his liquor. That's great. Whoa, you're a hero! Stupid idiot's what y'are."

That woman's voice came again, and then he was sitting out there at the piano, hearing himself sing. And then he was backstage again, only this time there were new people back there, not just that one fucking idiot from before. There was some scrawny girl and a long-haired boy from some rock-'n'-roll paper. And Elmo—he was there too. (Pappy had got himself married early last year, a few weeks after his seventieth birthday; married to a forty-seven-year-old Memphis lady, Lila May. But Pappy didn't like staying at home with Miss Lily. He liked flying from town to town, from bar to bar, with his son, drinking, telling tales, chasing down skirts.) Right now

Pappy was trying to tell a joke, a good one, but Jerry Lee would not cut loose of that heaven-and-hell stuff.

"Is there anything I haven't been through?" Jerry Lee asked himself aloud. "How many roads are left for me to travel? Am I livin' in my last an' final hour?"

" 'I'm just a hunnerd yards from Mary Ann . . .' " Elmo began to sing.

"Dr. Jekyll and Mr. Hyde! That's what that bitch always called me!" Jerry Lee snarled. Then he turned to the boy with the long hair and he said, "You know what armadillas are, boy?"

"Amarillo, Texas?"

"Hell, Louisiana's got more of 'em than Texas. Grave-robbers, them things. Git in them cheap coffins, start chewin', eat 'em up."

"They got little legs, a shell, and a keen nose," Elmo said, coming to the aid of the boy with the long hair.

"Like Myra," Jerry Lee said, letting his head drop back in hoarse laughter. Then he snapped his head forward and muttered, "I'd been a helluva lot better off if I'd married a damn armadilla. Naw, I take that back."

"How 'bout that night Jane was pregnant," Elmo hollered to his son. "You stuck that toothpick through that olive, said, 'Here y'are, Jane, look jes' like you.' "

"I believe that was Myra."

"Mighta been. I thought it was Jane."

"Never could keep up with Jane that good."

"Ya always useta call Myra a monkey," Elmo laughed. "Mama useta call me a giraffe, 'member? An' I called her a elephant."

"Yeah," Jerry Lee groaned, "them was *good* days. *Jokin'* days."

"Yup, we sure done our bit o' jokin', huh?"

"Them was good days."

"There was this contest at the zoo up in *Mon*roe," Elmo began to tell the boy with the long hair, "this contest t'name the giraffe. So—"

"Myra. I married her."

"I shoulda wrote in, my wife said, an'—"

"Thirteen-year-ol' cousin. *Chile bride.*"

"—name 'im Elmo! That woulda been a good name for that giraffe."

"She made her bed; she can lay in it."

"Yessir, good name for that ol' giraffe," Elmo laughed, pouring, then drinking.

"But I have a daughter by her. Got a son in the grave. This means *something*. But I don't know. . . . She walked in now and heard me call her an armadilla, ya'd see some action, I'll tell ya that."

"Is today Good Friday?" asked the girl, breaking her silence with sweet timidity.

"Good *what*?" Jerry Lee turned toward her.

"Good Friday?" she said, in an even softer voice.

"What's that mean?"

"That was the day Christ was crucified," she said.

"Now how you know that? You a Catholic? You talkin' about a horse of a differ'nt color. I ain't got nothin' against Catholics—I jes' wasn't raised up that way."

"Sunday's Easter, ain't it?" Elmo asked the girl.

"Nex' Sunday," Jerry Lee said.

"Then this isn't Good Friday," the boy with the long hair said.

"I didn't turn Catholic till I was sixteen," the girl offered.

"Easter," Jerry Lee said, then drank. Then he turned to the

boy with the long hair, and he said, "Why do you wear your hair like that? Do you know that it says in the Bible that it's a sin for a man to wear long hair?"

"I always thought Jesus had long hair," the boy said.

"*You thought.* It don't say nowhere in the Bible that Jesus had long hair. Ain't nobody knows what Christ looked like. It says nothin' about him havin' long hair, it says nothin' about him havin' a beard."

"I didn't think people had scissors in those days."

"Huh? What? They didn't? Where'd you git that shit from?"

"I don't know when scissors were invented, but . . ."

"Them Romans were pretty smart cats."

"Moses supposedly had a beard."

"Now you're goin' back some, son, way back. That Moses was a pretty old cat. Let's give him the benefit of the doubt. But we're not talkin' 'bout Moses, are we? We're talkin' 'bout *you.* Why d'you wanna wear your hair like a woman? Are you comfortable like that? What're you provin'?"

"I'm not proving anything."

"Yes you are. I mean, we got girls. We don't need damn men to look like girls. We need damn *men* to look like *men.* Hell, man, comb your hair back, style it, do *somethin'* with it. Look like you're s'posed to look. I just don't understand. What're you searchin' for? You're a nice-lookin' young man. Got a keen brain, a kind heart, I can tell that. Apparently you come from a good family. You don't have to . . . *hair hangin' down like a damn girl!* Why'n't you put you a damn *dress* on? Now, listen, I'm tellin' ya somethin' for your own good. You're a good person. I jes' can't . . . See, that's why I'm so successful in this business. I don't need to have hair hangin' down like a damn girl. Hell, I'm nearly thirty-eight years old. But I'm still hangin' in there, all the way. I got gumption, boy. I jes' can't see . . . *why* in the *hell* do you wanna look like a *woman? I don't like it, man!* But, what I don't . . . You still haven't answered my question: why is it necessary for you to wear your hair long?"

"Why is it necessary for you to play piano with your feet?"

"You're jumpin' way ahead, son. There ain't too many Jerry Lee Lewises in this world. There ain't but one. So let's get back to the hair. You think it looks good?"

"Yeah, I like the way I look."

"You look like shit."

"When my hair is your length, I—"

"Boy, you could never have hair like me. You ain't never born that way. You got a fine head of hair. You're a fine-lookin' young man. Get a damn haircut, man. Comb your hair right. Be a man. You people are searchin' for somethin'. I'd love to find out. *This long hair shit with a man is a bunch of motherfuckin' shit, and any sonofabitchin' man wears his hair like a woman has got a fuckin' weakness he'd better get rid of!* Downfall."

"I don't believe that."

"I don't give a fuck what you believe, boy. *Write that down in your fuckin' black book!*"

Then dawn broke.

It was August 26, and Jerry Lee and the band had just flown home from a show in New York. They had landed at about one o'clock in the morning. Jerry Lee wanted to roar.

"We were real wired up and raving around the city," Tarp Tarrant remembered. "We had been in several joints and the Killer had almost gotten into a fight in every place. We finally went down to Overton Square, to TGI Friday's. We had just sat down and they were playing Jerry Lee Lewis records over the loudspeakers. At the table next to ours were two couples from Arkansas. The two men were giants, and their old ladies were hogs. After a few minutes, the men got up and went to the restroom. At that time, one of the ladies said, 'I hate this Jerry Lee Lewis shit they're playin'.' The Killer just turned around and said, 'Fuck you, you old redneck whore!' and turned back around.

"About two minutes later, a man tapped Jerry on the shoulder and said, 'Are you Jerry Lee Lewis?' The Killer said, 'The one and only.' The man hit him and broke his nose. We were so stoned we didn't think it was broken. I told Jerry to let me take him to the doctor, but he said, 'Hell, no, man, I'm rockin'! Besides, ain't nobody can hurt the Killer—I'm all right.'

"Nine hours passed, and we had gone to several other clubs. By this time, Jerry's nose had swollen up real big, and he let us take him to Baptist Hospital. He just laughed and said, 'One more battle scar won't matter none.' He was laid up in the hospital for a week."

At 1:45 in the dark, cold morning of October 17, Memphis patrolmen J. P. Barker and L. L. Howeth were directing traffic at the scene of an accident at the intersection of Democrat Road and Airways Boulevard, not far from the offices of Jerry Lee Lewis Enterprises, Inc.

They saw a Lincoln Continental heading toward them, swerving from one side of the road to the other, and they halted it. The Killer rolled his window down and tried to address the patrolmen, but the words came out crooked. He was taken away and made to blow into an Intoximeter. He registered .15. The police at the station were impressed, for many of them had never known the device to register beyond .10.

Jerry Lee had given Junior the jeep for his nineteenth birthday. Now, eleven days later, November 13, Junior fitted a tow bar to the rear of the jeep and drove from Memphis to DeSoto

County, Mississippi, to fetch another car, a Ford XL, from a repair shop. He was driving back along Holly Springs Road, near Hernando, at about eight-thirty that evening. He turned. The Ford that he was towing swerved around and hit the abutment of a bridge. It jackknifed and overturned the jeep. He was pronounced dead at 9:24 P.M.

Jerry Lee claimed the body of his son, and he had the hospital people put it in a rubber sack. He took the sack to his plane, and he laid it in the aisle of the plane, and he told his pilot to steer south, toward Ferriday.

"When Junior died," Eddie Kilroy recalled, "Jerry sent the plane to Nashville to pick up my wife, Maria, and I, and take us to Ferriday. Maria got spooked on the plane. She thought the plane was evil, because of Jerry Lee. Then we hit a buzzard on the way down. That spooked both of us. We were comin' in on approach, and this big black buzzard broke right through the glass into the cockpit. If it had happened at a higher altitude, we woulda had some bad trouble."

Services were held on November 15 at the Church of God. The preacher spoke of the soon coming of the Lord, and an elderly woman rose and gave a message in tongues. Then Jerry Lee Lewis, Jr., was taken to his place in the little cemetery near Clayton. Jerry Lee told the man that he wanted a heart-shaped tombstone placed over the grave, and on that stone heart he wanted there to be carved a drum and words of pride.

HIS LIFE WAS GENTLE, AND THE ELEMENTS SO MIX'D IN HIM, THAT NATURE MIGHT STAND UP AND SAY TO ALL THE WORLD, "THIS WAS A MAN!"

Both his sons had been taken from him. He himself was now the final son, the last Lewis in this tale that had begun in Monroe almost two hundred years ago, and he was fated to bring the tale to its end, with no male issue to carry it further, or even to retell it. With him, the fine name of his unconquerable forebears would cease to be.

But no matter. He would end the tale, and he would end it good, and he would burn toward that end with all the somber glories of all the Lewises that had ever lived in all the tales his daddy had ever told him; and long after there was no one left to remember Judge Lewis or Old Man Lewis or Leroy or Elmo, long after the memory of those men had become part of the dirt and the sky and the floods and the sadness—long after that, the name of the final wild son would live on; he swore it.

On December 3, three weeks after Jerry Lee had laid his son beneath the ground, his wife, Jaren, filed a Circuit Court suit seeking separate maintenance and child support. She accused Jerry Lee of cruel and inhuman treatment and said that she and he had recently separated again.

A month later, on January 7, 1974, his bass player, Hawk Hawkins, and his steel guitarist, Charlie Owens, quit and filed suit against him for $8,000 in back salaries.

Jerry Lee Lewis Enterprises, Inc., the company he had started little more than a year before, fell into disorganization and debt. He was evicted from his suite of offices on Airways Boulevard and sued by the owner of the building.

The previous spring he had agreed to give a two-hour concert at the University of Virginia, but had left the stage after only twenty minutes. Now, a year later, on May 3, a judge found him guilty of breach of contract and ordered him to pay $10,625 to the university.

He turned on his car radio, and he heard Mickey Gilley's name—pronounced not the way it had been back in Ferriday, with a soft *G,* but with a hard *G*—and then he heard his cousin singing "Room Full of Roses," and he heard the disc jockey say that Mickey Gilley sounded a lot like Jerry Lee Lewis and that this was because Mickey and Jerry Lee were first cousins and had been raised up together, learning to play on the same piano; and he shut the radio off.

Mickey Gilley's record "Room Full of Roses" became a Number One country hit in June, 1974. The record was produced by Eddie Kilroy, who later said, "We did a lot of publicity about how Mickey couldn't help but play like Jerry Lee, them comin' up together in Ferriday, that sorta shit. Mickey worked hard to sound like Jerry Lee."

After "Room Full of Roses," Mickey had another Number One country hit, "I Overlooked an Orchid"; and after that he had another Number One country hit, "City Lights." Three Number One records in a single year. This was something that Jerry Lee had never done. He had not even had a Number One record in more than two years. In 1974 he had gone into the studio four times, and the highest any of his records had gone up the country charts was to Number Eight. His albums weren't doing anything either. Jimmy Lee Swaggart's gospel albums were selling better than his albums.

In October, the Cappaert Investment Corporation filed suit against Jerry Lee for $100,838 he owed in payments on the Convair turbojet he had bought three years before.

Enlaced in chaos and ancient night, he opened the Bible and read of the demons, how they were cast into the swine, how the swine ran violently down a steep place into the sea, and how they perished in the water.

It was 1975. It might just as well have been 1965. He took a drink and beheld himself in the mirror. There were lines on his face that he had never seen before. He looked for the eyes of the hawk, but saw only his own, pink and milky from the wages of unclean succor. The hair, though, the hair—the hair was yet of majesty.

The Convair flew in from Vancouver and landed in Denver on the morning of February 25. As the plane rolled to a halt, Jerry Lee looked out the plastic pane and saw several men in government duds. They were armed, and two of them had strange-looking black dogs on leashes. There were three other men, wearing dark blue suits, white shirts, and blood-red ties.

The dogs and the men in the suits discovered most of the drugs that were on the plane. Jerry Lee and the twelve others aboard the plane were taken to the courthouse in downtown Denver, where they were individually interrogated about an international drug ring they knew nothing about.

That night armed policemen stood by the stage of the Denver club were Jerry Lee pumped and howled, and they did this every night for a week, until Jerry Lee and his boys left town.

On March 11 he performed at Bad Bob's Lounge in Memphis. He began arguing with a girl at the club, and he eventually ended up taking a fiddle bow to her. The girl, claiming that she was "brutally and savagely attacked," filed suit against him, seeking $100,000 in damages. A judge eventually fined him twenty-five dollars for striking the complainant, then fined the complainant fifteen dollars for breaking the bow.

A month later, on April 11, Jaren filed for divorce, claiming that Jerry Lee had threatened her with bodily harm.

On Saturday, June 19, Jerry Lee went into the Mercury studio in Nashville and, with a voice of pained torpor, recorded a song that had recently been written for him by Donnie Fritts, a member of Kris Kristofferson's band. It was called "A Damn Good Country Song."

Well, I took enough pills for the whole damn town;
Jerry Lee Lewis drank enough whiskey to lift any ship off of
   the ground.
I'll be the first to admit it;
I sure wish that these people would quit it,
'Cause it's tough enough to straighten up when they won't leave
   you alone.
My life would make a damn good country song.

He came upon Elvis in Las Vegas, and he said to Elvis, "You don't know what you're doin'. You're just Colonel Parker's puppet."

"Well," said Elvis, "if I'm so dumb and you're so smart, how is it that I'm playin' the main room and you're playin' the lounge?"

It seemed to him that he had been sued by everyone and his mother. He was getting used to it. But he never expected that he might be sued by a dead man.

He had been performing in Atlanta on the night of November 3, 1968, when some fucking idiot made a comment about one of his songs. So he had taken his microphone stand and hit the idiot in the face with it. Now, seven years later, in Decem-

237

ber, 1975, he was being sued by the estate of this idiot, who had died in 1970. The suit was for $30,000 in damages to cover medical expenses that the late idiot had incurred in treating the injury to his left eye that had been caused by that mike stand of wrath. This was a new one on the Killer, and he sort of relished it for that moment before he disregarded it.

"A Damn Good Country Song" had not been a hit. It had barely made it onto the country charts. On December 15 he returned to the studio and he cut five songs. One of these was a long version of Billy Swan's 1974 hit, "I Can Help." Midway through a languid piano break, he growled, "Think about it, Elvis." He ended the session by commanding the musicians to get the hell out of the studio. Nothing he recorded that day was deemed suitable for release by Mercury.

On the night of December 27, while performing at the Executive Inn in Evansville, Indiana, he paused between songs to take a sip. "You're lookin' at a livin' legend," he said, and then fell silent for a moment. "Y'know, that really worries me. I always thought a legend was somethin' dead." And then he recommenced the Devil's boogie.

Blue-and-gold, blue-and-gold, blue-and-gold.

On February 10, 1976, Jerry Lee entered St. Joseph Hospital in Memphis, for treatment of "influenza and a nasal problem." He was released two weeks later, on the 28th.

Five days after Jerry Lee entered the hospital, Tarp Tarrant, his drummer, got into his 1966 Cutlass Oldsmobile and began to drive.

Los Angeles, 1977, with sister Linda Gail on the tambourine.

"I was just drivin' around. I was bored, I was upset, I was high. My wife and kids were out of groceries. We were out of propane. A few days before Jerry had gone into the hospital, I had asked him for some money. He owed me five or six grand. He said he didn't have it.

"I was in a bad way. I was doin' Placidyl and amphetamines, Biphetamines, Dexedrine, snortin' a lot of cocaine, and drinkin' wine and Jack Daniel's all week. This particular night I had taken seven or eight Black Widows, and I was drinkin' beer.

"I kept my pistol in the car. It was a little old .22 target pistol, nine-shot revolver. I drove by this store, the Seven-Eleven on Highland. I saw this girl in there by herself, behind the counter. Everything just sorta snapped—just like that; it was like I had been needin' some money and I had a gun in the car. So I just pulled up there, y'know. It was a real stupid thing, because I was so high, and I was wearin' a Stetson cowboy hat, a black leather suit, black boots with spurs. I had my gun tied down, all this crap. I backed the car up in there where she could see the license plate. Left the car runnin'. Walked in there dressed up like Lash LaRue. It was just really a crazy scene, I didn't even think about what the hell I was doin', man, 'cause if I had I wouldn't't've done it.

"I got fifty-eight bucks.

"I got back in the car, turned left off Highland, comin' up Central, headin' into Memphis, doin' eighty miles an hour in a forty-mile zone. A squad car passed me. Turned out that the APB was out and there was a six-car roadblock set up farther down on Central. I smashed right into it, knocked a squad car over. They dropped down eight or nine shotguns on me, started screamin' 'Get out of the car!' I was wavin' my pistol around. Some rookie ran up the side of the car, grabbed me by the collar—I still had the gun in my hand—and he hit me over the head with the butt end of his shotgun.

"I got eight to ten."

Jerry Lee turned on the TV, and he saw Jimmy Lee Swaggart pacing back and forth with a handkerchief in his hand, scowling, preaching of the evils of the flesh, asking himself questions, then answering them.

"You mean you think it's wrong for a lady to wear shorts?

"Yes! Yes! Yes!

"Lady, your body is the temple of the Holy Ghost!"

The Bible mentioned many demons by name. But how many were there who possessed no names? How many were there for every shade of darkness that passed through every moment of every night since the beginning of time? He threw water on his face, and he thought of Dorothy, the preacher's daughter, and of her neck.

On April 12 Jerry Lee was sued by the Franklin Development and Investment Company, who sought $8,108 in unpaid rent on two town houses he had leased the previous summer.

Jimmy Lee had begun sending him copies of his magazine, *The Evangelist*. Every issue, in the column "Brother Swaggart, Here Is My Question," Jimmy Lee took a stand on a moral problem posed by a reader.

Question: Is oral–genital sex scripturally permissive between husband and wife?
Answer: No, I don't think so. I realize the Bible says the

marriage bed is undefiled (Hebrews 13:4), but the Holy Spirit certainly did not mean uncleanliness or perversion.

On May 20, and again on May 28, he went into the studio in Nashville. These were his only recording sessions of the year: a sum of eight songs. In all the years since 1957, he had never cut so little. His contract with Mercury would end the following year, and he began to wonder.

His reputation had fallen so low in the last few years that the editor of his fan club newsletter, *The Rebel,* was prompted to write:

> Jerry Lee has earned many times over the right for respect. Nobody has ever paid a higher price for that respect! When someone is appointed or takes it upon themselves to represent Jerry Lee, they should show full dignity and loyalty!!
>
> I firmly believe the world would be a far better place if some people in it would learn to control their mouth's instead of the nack of wheeling the perverable knife.

"There's very few great talents left," he told Todd Everett, who was interviewing him for Earth News Radio this hot night of August 17 backstage at the Palomino Club in North Hollywood. "You got Elvis Presley, Chuck Berry, Charlie Rich, B. B. King. I'm not sayin' that I'm one of 'em—I'm sayin' that *I'm the main one.*"

The interviewer asked him about his influences.

"*No way.* You'll never find anyone that Jerry Lee Lewis has taken anything from, brother. I'm a *stylist.* Jes' like Jimmie Rodgers—the late, great Jimmie Rodgers—jes' like Hank Williams—late, great Hank Williams—jes' like Al Jolson—the late, great Al Jolson. There's only four stylists, and that's

Jerry Lee Lewis, Hank Williams, Al Jolson, and Jimmie Rodgers. Rest of 'em are jes' . . . *imitators*."

The interviewer asked him about his private life.

"Private life? I have no private life. My life's an open book, always has been."

"What's the best record you ever made?"

"Let's git back on the private life. I have no private life. I cover up nothin', I hide nothin'. I many not be right—I *know* I'm wrong—but I'll be the first to admit it. And I wanna say this to the folks out in radioland: Jerry Lee Lewis is a *sinner,* lost an' undone, without God *or* His Son. I will be the first one to admit it."

"I understand that Jimmy Lee Swaggart is your cousin."

"Double first cousin. His daddy's my daddy's nephew, his mother was my mother's sister. We learned to play on the same piano. Mickey, too."

"To get back to my earlier question, what's the best record you ever made?"

"Let's git back to Mickey. I think he's had it. Him and Jimmy, they don't have the depths that I have. Swear to God, they don't. I told 'em at my grandmother's funeral, I said, 'Boys, y'all have got a lot of talent. But *God* blessed *me* with the *talent;* y'all jes' got the scrapin's.' Mickey got a little upset about it. Jimmy Lee jes' fell down laughin'. He's a Christian boy. Great preacher, Holy Ghost field. Oh, man, he's somethin' else. Never changed since he's fifteen."

"Do you go back to Ferriday very often?"

"No, not anymore. I have some people back there, but not like my mama, who is passed away, my two sons, who have passed away. There's really nothin' there for me anymore; it's jes' bad memories. I'll be buried there someday, if God's willin'."

"Are you a churchgoing person?"

"I useta be."

"What stopped you?"

"Satan, I would imagine, out of the weakness of Jerry Lee Lewis. I'm one of the most weakest people in the world when it comes to religion. No such thing as religion, anyway. The Bible don't even speak of religion—it's *salvation.* I was sanctified at one time, and a great Christian person. I'm fixin' to git back into it. Fixin' to quit this business, son, git back into workin' for the Lord. If I don't, I've had it. I gotta devote my life to God, git back in the ministry. That's the only way. God said He would rather have you hot or cold, for if you are lukewarm He'll spew you out of His mouth. *Think about it, darlin'!* I was at one time a great preacher."

"You're a great preacher now."

"But what a failure. Forty-one years old. It's sad. Cost me two sons and my mother."

"How was that your fault?"

"Hardheaded Lewis. I have been the hardheadedest cat that's ever been. It's a shame. I don't know *why, why* I'm that way. It's drainin' my body dry. I don't understand, I don't know *why* I'm not man enough to walk out that door an' do what I'm s'posed to do, 'cause if I don't I'm gonna go to hell. I really don't *know,* man, what's *wrong* with me. What am I doin' here, in a *nightclub*? I can't give an altar call here. This won't git me to heaven. When I stand before God—and they *shall* stand before Him, great and small, and give account according to the deeds that they've done; they'll say, Lord, I have cast out devils in Thy name, done many works, many wonders, in Thy name; He'll say, Depart from Me, you workers of iniquity, *I* never knew you.

"Jesus died for us. God expects—talkin' 'bout God, not Jesus—God expects *loyalty,* and if He don't git it, go with the

one ya served on earth, which is the man that has power next
to God, which is *Satan,* which has power more than Jesus. He
tempted Him for forty days and forty nights, *and he nearly got
'im."*

"Are you currently married?"

"Getting a divorce. This is it for me, there's no more. Can't
marry anymore. I'm through. *I will not* . . . And I do believe
that if I go back into the ministry, God intends for me to be by
myself."

"Doesn't the response of the crowds bring you *some* happiness?"

"Satan. He got power next to God. He'll drag you . . . to
the . . . depths of . . . of agony."

"How does Satan benefit from your entertaining people?"

" 'Cause I'm draggin' the audience to hell with me. How
am I gonna git 'em to heaven with 'Whole Lotta Shakin' Goin'
On'? You can't serve two masters; you'll hate one an' love the
other."

Little more than a month later, on the afternoon of September 29, Jerry Lee's forty-first birthday, his bass player of three
years, Norman "Butch" Owens, visited Jerry Lee and Jaren at
435 Cardinal, where Jaren had taken up residence. He brought
with him a copy of Jerry Lee's new album, *Country Class,*
which had been released a few days before.

The two men sat drinking and talking, while Jaren watched
TV in the living room. Jerry Lee pulled out a .357 Magnum
and pointed it toward Owens.

"Look down the barrel of this," he said. Then he aimed the
gun to the right of Owens and said, "I'm gonna shoot that
Coca-Cola bottle over there or my name ain't Jerry Lee Lewis."
Then there was gunfire.

Owens clutched the two bleeding holes in his chest and stumbled into the living-room. Jaren hollered at him for bleeding on her new white carpet.

Owens was taken to St. Joseph Hospital, where he underwent emergency surgery. Jerry Lee was charged with shooting a firearm inside the city limits, a misdemeanor.

Two weeks later, on the evening of October 12, Jerry Lee was arrested at Jaren's house and charged with disorderly conduct. He had been standing outside shouting obscenities at Jaren's neighbors. He posted the fifty-dollar bond, returned home, and continued drinking.

At nine in the morning on November 22, he steered his $46,000 Rolls-Royce onto Powell Road, and he kept steering into the turn as if it had never happened, and the Rolls flipped over and tumbled into a ditch. He crawled out. The police were already there, and they took him to jail. He registered zero on the Intoximeter, but, according to police chief H. A. Goforth, "His tongue seemed thick. His eyes were bloodshot, and he was kind of unsteady on his feet."

Less than twelve hours later, Elmo was arrested near Robinsonville, Mississippi, and charged with speeding and driving while intoxicated. He refused to take an alcohol-content test and was put in the Tunica County Jail.

Ten hours after Jerry Lee was released from jail, he drove to Graceland, to the two-leaved gate. He waved his pistol, and he cursed the night.

It was his second arrest in two days. After being released, he entered Doctors' Hospital, on the evening of November 25.

Purportedly he was treated for influenza and a peptic ulcer. His wife, Jaren, entered St. Joseph's Hospital that same day, for treatment of "nerves."

On Sunday morning, December 5, Jimmy Lee Swaggart made a televised plea for the salvation of his cousin's soul.

"I want to dedicate this next hymn," he said, "to a troubled relative. I don't want to embarrass him, but you all know him. He's Jerry Lee Lewis.

"Jerry and I are very close. He's having a lot of trouble these days, and I hope that in some way this might help. It's called 'Now I Have Everything.' "

In Nashville a few days later, Swaggart told a *Banner* columnist that "I almost hate to answer the phone sometimes because I know somebody is going to tell me Jerry is dead."

Jerry Lee returned to Doctors' Hospital the following month, on January 17. Two days later, his gall bladder was removed. A European tour, which had been scheduled to begin on February 10, was canceled.

On May 2 St. Joseph Hospital filed suit against him seeking $3,425 in unpaid bills.

He put on righteousness as a breastplate and lifted the bottle to his lips, and he told his dwindling myrmidons once again of Old Man Lewis and his horse-felling fist. The dwindling myrmidons praised and adored him and brought to his lips replenishment—blue-and-gold pills and amber whiskey.

Jimmy Lee Swaggart raised his handkerchief to his temple, and he closed his eyes and shouted:

"The answer is not psychiatry!"

"The answer is not psychology!
"The answer is not therapy!
"The answer is the Spirit of God!"

On the afternoon of June 22, Jerry Lee was seized by police while swerving fast down Highway 72 in a white Rolls-Royce. He was placed under arrest, charged with driving while under the influence of drugs.

It was August 16, and Elvis was dead, face down on his bathroom floor. If only he had listened that night; listened and learned of the two masters and of the sword of the whore-hating Ghost.

A thunderstorm crossed Tennessee that afternoon. Two days later, police officers stood in solemnity along Elvis Presley Boulevard and saluted as the white Cadillac hearse rolled slowly by. They, the Killer's persecutors, saluted.

They sat in a motel room in Nashville. It was fall, but it was still hot.

"How did you react to Elvis Presley's death?" the man from the country music magazine asked him.

"I was glad. Just another one outa the way. I mean, Elvis this, Elvis that. All we hear is Elvis. What the shit did Elvis do except take dope that I couldn't git ahold of? That's very discouraging, anybody that had that much power to git ahold of that much dope. All I did was drink whiskey.

"You expect me to sit here and tell a lie about something? Look, we've only got one life to live. We don't have the promise of the next breath. I know what I am. I'm a rompin', stompin', piano-playin' sonofabitch. A *mean* sonofabitch. But a great sonofabitch. A good person. Never hurt nobody unless they got in my way. I got a mean streak in me. Elvis did, too. He hid his. I don't hide mine. I gotta lay it open sometimes.

"*Elvis*. That sonofabitch died on dope. His heart was twice the size as normal. That's how much dope he took. I'm tellin' you what he done. He was a dope addict. I am an alcoholic."

"Anything you would like to tell your fans?" the man from the country music magazine asked.

"Yeah. Kiss my ass. If they don't buy my records, they can bark my hole. And if they don't buy my albums, they can use my dick for a walkin' pole. God, that was awful. Erase that. Naw, I'll tell ya what I think of my fans. I think of them exactly the way they think about me."

In September, Butch Owens, the bass player whom Jerry Lee had shot in the chest a year before, had filed a suit against the Killer and his estranged wife, Jaren, seeking $400,000 in punitive and compensatory damages. Jerry Lee refused to appear in court. On December 8 his disgruntled attorney, Warner Hodges III, asked for and was granted permission to be dismissed from the case.

On December 14–15 he went into the studio and cut fifteen songs. These were the last records he would make for Mercury. Soon he would have a new label, Elektra. It didn't matter, except for the advance.

At one in the afternoon, February 23, Jerry Lee was rushed to the emergency room of Baptist Hospital, suffering from respiratory distress.

Soon after he arrived at the hospital, reports flooded the Memphis newspapers and TV stations. Jerry Lee Lewis, these reports said, was dead.

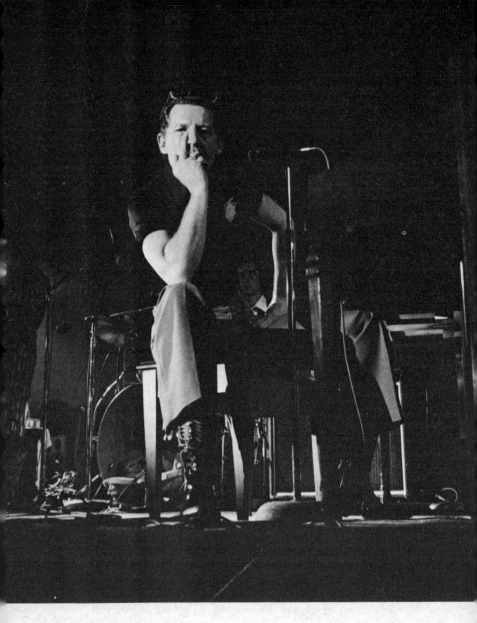

Austin, August, 1976.

On the evening of April 1, he walked onto the stage of the Old South Jamboree in Walker, Louisiana, and he beheld those who had assembled before him: whoremongers and idolaters, Saducees and freethinkers, dick-sucking blondes and slaves of Mammon—all manner of filth born of the flesh of woman. He seated himself unsteadily at the piano, but he did not make music. When the crowd grew restive, he stood and kicked his stool into their midst.

"Y'all *paid* for this," he taunted into the microphone. The filth uttered cries of censure and of confusion. He was their god, and he was abandoning them. Without him, through whom they vicariously blazed, they were doomed to the insignificance and sameness of their lives in this gelt, assimilated South, which they in their drab and petty greed had fashioned from the brave new world of their forebears.

"Kiss my ass!" he commanded, savoring the impotent uproar with which his words were met. "You sonofabitches think you got somethin' comin' just 'cause you pay a few dollars for a goddamn ticket. Shit, I'll sing when I'm good and fuckin' ready. Anybody don't like it, them doors swing both ways."

The crowd rose and seemed about to riot, but the god of their betrayal fell unconscious and was removed from the stage, and they, as they had feared, were left alone.

James Hodges, the promoter of the show, filed a suit against Jerry Lee, and eventually, on February 21, 1980, the Killer was ordered to pay $8,220 in damages.

On May 3 he was fined two hundred dollars and given a thirty-day suspended sentence for his most recent driving-while-drugged conviction. After placing him on a year's probation, Criminal Court Judge William H. Williams said:

"You have a God-given talent and you should be paying closer attention to the drugs you are taking. When Presley died he had thirteen different drugs in his system.

"You, Jerry Lee Lewis, are somebody special. But the only way you can protect your talent is to back up and take a look at your life and what you are doing with it.

"This is your third conviction on a charge of driving while under the influence of alcohol or drugs. If you get yourself in shape, you can still be the great international performer you've always been."

On his forty-third birthday, he dreamed of that stillness long ago. The little stone lamb spoke and shrieked.

The United States of America had been filing federal tax liens against Jerry Lee since that fateful May of 1958. "In all the years that he was with Mercury, he never collected any royalties from his records," Jerry Kennedy recalled. "He was just livin' on performances. Any royalties that he earned went directly toward the liens. Still do, I assume, although he was in an unearned position when he left here to go with Elektra."

The liens had grown greater and greater. On May 12, nine days after Jerry Lee had been placed on probation by Judge Williams, the government had filed a lien against him for $80,328.25; then, barely six months later, on November 14, it filed another lien against him, for $84,764.87. The sum of the various federal liens was in excess of $274,000.

On February 26, 1979, agents of the Internal Revenue Service obtained from the United States District Court in Oxford, Mississippi, a writ of entry to the Killer's ranch. On the next day, the agents arrived at his Malone Road address with a fleet of eight tow trucks they had requisitioned from Newt's

Wrecker Service in nearby Hernando. The agents seized Jerry Lee's five motorcycles, two Lincoln Continentals, and Corvette Stingray; his 1935 Ford sedan, his 1941 Ford convertible, and his 1954 black-and-gold Cadillac; his jeep and even his tractor. They also seized a new $68,000 Rolls-Royce, but it developed that the Rolls-Royce dealership in Memphis had laid a previous claim to the car, for nonpayment.

As the tow trucks hauled the vehicles away, the federal men entered the Killer's house and, before his glaring eyes, slowly gathered his worldly possessions: his arsenal of twenty-two rifles and handguns; his diamond rings, gold wristwatches, and silver bracelets; rare coins from the times of the tales; stereo equipment and television sets; musical instruments and furniture. These things, along with the vehicles, were transported by the agents across the state line and placed in the Aero Customs Bonded Warehouse in Memphis.

"They treated me like a dog," he told a reporter from the United Press International. "They just came to my house and didn't even knock, just took away my cars and didn't leave me one. They shouldn't oughta done that. They should've come to me like men and said, 'Jerry Lee, you owe us some money.' Then we could've worked somethin' out."

He stood in his front yard beneath the cold gray sky, and he looked out across his land, breathing slowly, sternly, and shaking his head. Like Old Man Lewis before him, he was left now with nothing but the dirt and the courage.

"I don't think they'll ever bring my stuff back," he said, hearing not so much his own words as the breath in the wind of that other, brooding century—that breath that now conspired in sunless harmony with his own. "And I don't care if they don't. I'll go out and git me some more."

On March 13 he departed for a two-week engagement in Las Vegas. Not long after his arrival, it became obvious that he was in no condition to perform, and he was checked into a hospital.

By Sunday, March 25, he was back in Mississippi. Two De Soto County reserve deputies were driving down Pleasant Hill Road that morning when Jerry Lee passed them at a high speed in a 1979 white Corvette that had been leased for him by his latest wench. A few minutes later, the deputies found the Corvette in a ditch on the right-hand side of a left-hand curve in the road, about two miles from Jerry Lee's ranch. The deputies looked at the 150-foot skid marks that the Corvette had burned onto the road, then they looked through the cracked windshield of the car; but there was nothing within.

He turned the worn, familiar pages to the Book of Job, to the words, "He hath swallowed down riches, and he shall vomit them up again: God shall cast them out of his belly."

He filed for a divorce from Jaren that spring, accusing her of "habitual, cruel, and inhuman treatment" and claiming that he and she had "not cohabitated as husband and wife since October 21, 1971."

On June 8 Jaren filed a countersuit, charging him with "cruel and inhuman treatment, adultery, habitual drunkenness, and habitual use of drugs."

Was it not true, after all, that women dreamed of intercourse with the Devil?

Elmo Kidd Lewis was seventy-seven and still grinning when he entered Doctors' Hospital in Memphis on June 11, 1979. It was a hot day, and he spoke of that to the nurses and to the black orderlies.

A week later, on June 18, Jerry Lee sat onstage at the Palomino Club in North Hollywood, and he looked into the eyes of his audience and said, "Elvis killed himself over a broad. It took five of 'em to put me in the shape I'm in today."

In his dressing room after the show he sat, holding in his lap a half-drained quart of Seagram's like the unglowing scepter of an ancient, fading kingship. He drew on his cigar and gestured toward the tape recorder that a writer had placed before him.

"Y'know, one o' them things can git a man killed," he said. "A man be drinkin', sayin' somethin', somebody take that tape an' use it against 'im. Git 'im buried."

"The time is near," he said, his eyes wide, as in terror, regarding every mote that drifted through the stale air of that dressing room as if it held innumerable demons. "We don't have the promise of the next breath. Fire and brimstone. The fire never dies, the burnin' never dies; the fire never quenches, for the weeping, wailing, gnashing of teeth."

"Is anybody going to heaven?" the writer asked him.

"Very few, very few. It's a hard place to git to, son. Can't git there through the Palomino Club, that's for sure. Church can't git you to heaven. Religion can't git you to heaven." Then he took a good long swig, and he changed the subject. "Y'know, son," he said, "there's only been four of us: Al Jolson, Jimmie Rodgers, Hank Williams, and Jerry Lee Lewis. That's your only four fuckin' stylists that ever lived. We could write, sing, yodel, dance, fuck, or what—makes no damn difference. The rest of these idiots is either ridin' a fuckin' horse, pickin' a gittar, or shootin' somebody in some stupid damn movie." Then he took another swig and yelled, "Next!"

255

"How do you feel about people who combine music and politics?"

"Buncha fuckin' idiots."

"So you don't figure on playing at any antinuke benefits in the near future?"

"Hell, no. Fuck 'em all! Fuck 'em! Blow 'em all clear to hell! Shit, git it over quick. Jes' don't kill no alligators in Louisiana. I married a couple of 'em."

"You've been married five times now. Do—"

"That's my fuckin' business."

"Do you know any more about women now than you did the first time you got married?"

"Yeah. Pussy is pussy."

"Why are you so very obsessed with hell?"

"Because Satan has power next to God. You ain't loyal to God, you must be loyal to Satan. There ain't no in-between. Can't serve two gods. I'm a sinner, I know it. Soon I'm gonna have to reckon with the chillin' hands of death."

The summer days passed, and Elmo felt himself grow weaker. He began to suspect that he would never leave the hospital; but the moment he began to suspect this, he ceased to allow himself to suspect it. Not because he was a fool or a coward, no, but because he was Elmo Kidd Lewis, the tallest, toughest, grinningest, workingest sonofabitch that Snake Ridge, Louisiana, ever knew.

People came to visit with him, and he told them all about what he was planting this year and that if they wanted to find out what a good English pea really tasted like, then they should drop by to see him roundabout the second week in September, and don't forget the jug; and then he'd wink.

But he was wasting away, and he did not need any doctor boy to tell him that what had eaten his daddy's stomach back in '37 was now eating his. He thought of all the floods and of all the rare happiness, and of all the untellable wonder and sighing-ember sadness at the edge of Turtle Lake, and of the egrets there. And when there was almost nothing left of him, he let go. It was July 21, and it was still hot.

Jerry Lee took what was left of Elmo to Ferriday, to the Church of God, then to the quiet dirt near Clayton. People came up and put their arms around Jerry Lee, but he did not recognize these people, not even Johnny Littlejohn from the fine wild days across the river—not even his own sister Frankie Jean. Johnny and Frankie looked to one another in sadness.

"Ya know whose funeral we're gonna be goin' to next?" Johnny whispered.

"Yeah," Frankie Jean answered, looking as if to cry.

Jerry Lee stood there, looking at the tombstones and at the soil. They were all down there now, those from whom he had come. All of them—even old Calhoun. And now Pappy. All the life he had ever known, it was down there. He did not feel now like a part of the tales. He felt like nothing; worse, like something left behind.

On September 11, after Jerry Lee's repeated failure to appear in court, Judge Robert M. McRae, Jr., of the United States District Court in Memphis, ordered the absent and defaulted defendant and his estranged wife, Jaren, to pay $125,000 in damages to Butch Owens, who, three Septembers ago, had been told by his employer to "look down the barrel of this."

Seven days later, Internal Revenue Service agents returned to the Killer's ranch in Nesbit to claim more of his worldly possessions. After leaving the ranch, the agents reported to De Soto County Sheriff Denver "Dink" Sowell that quantities of controlled substances were to be found secreted in a certain place in the Killer's home.

He was arrested at noon the next day. Ordered to appear the following afternoon for a preliminary hearing at the De Soto County Court House, he was released on a $3,000 bond.

Wearing a silk ascot and smoking a corncob pipe, he told a reporter from the Associated Press that the bust had been a set-up. Asked about the current state of his career, the Killer told the reporter that he would soon be embarking on a concert tour of Saudi Arabia.

He drank and he lay down in darkness, like those that had long been dead. He was taken to a hospital in Memphis, and there he entered his forty-fourth year. His kin worried for his life. They spoke among themselves of having him committed to an asylum, but none of them, neither Frankie Jean nor Linda Gail, Jimmy Lee nor Mickey, dared to sign the necessary papers.

On October 1, Mickey Gilley flew his Cessna 210 from Pasadena, Texas, to Memphis. His wife, Vivian, had tried to discourage him from the flight. "You only got two days off," she had said, "and here you gonna be flyin', three hours to get there, four hours to get back—be gone all day and all night."

"I got to say that I tried," Mickey told his wife. "I don't wanna be sittin' back sayin', well, had I went maybe he'd be alive today."

The eyes that stared back at Mickey's eyes in Memphis that afternoon were eyes that he had never seen, eyes that avowed the unspeakable.

"Jerry," he said to those eyes. "What are you tryin' to do? Are you tryin' to destroy yourself? Is that what you want? Do you want to die? Because that's what's gonna happen. You're gonna kill yourself. You can't keep doin' what you're doin' to yourself and expect to go on livin'. It's not gonna happen. We'll end up buryin' you just like they did Elvis if you don't get off it. You're gonna die."

"Hell, no," the Killer said, "I wanna live, Mickey. I wanna live."

Jimmy Lee Swaggart clutched his Bible, wiped his neck with his white handkerchief, and peered into the TV camera.

" 'Jerry,' I said, 'why do you drink? Why do you take the pills? Why, Jerry, why?' And he looked at me, and there was pain in his eyes, and guilt, and he said to me: 'Those coffins keep passin' by me.' Do you hear that, people? 'Those coffins keep passin' by.' "

On Saturday night, November 24, the Killer locked himself in his dressing room backstage at the Orpheum Theatre in Memphis, where he was scheduled to perform at eight o'clock. Outside his door, United States marshals, armed with a writ of attachment, ordered him to unbolt the lock. The marshals had been instructed to seize all monies held by or on behalf of the Killer, along with any jewelry and musical equipment in his possession, in an attempt to satisfy the $125,000 court judgment that had been delivered against him in the Owens case.

Whenever the marshals spoke through the door to him, he commenced singing. " 'Just rollin' along with the tumblin' tumbleweeds. . . .' " At 10:20 the marshals finally withdrew, and Jerry Lee strode to the stage, introduced to the cheering, ravenous crowd as "the man the FBI wants, the IRS wants, and the U.S. marshals want—but you've got him! The Killer!"

On January 15, 1980, Dr. George Nichopoulos sat before the Tennessee Board of Medical Examiners in the Memphis City Council Chambers, defending himself against charges,

brought against him by the Board of Health, that he had pre-
scribed massive doses of addictive drugs for the late Elvis Presley and numerous other patients. Among those other patients
was listed Jerry Lee Lewis.

The white-haired Dr. Nichopoulos told the board that Jerry
Lee was a drug addict and that he had been hospitalized for his
addiction on at least three occasions since 1977. He said that
Jerry Lee customarily took eight or ten capsules of amphet-
amine before every performance.

"He was getting them off the streets," the doctor said. "I
was trying to control what he was taking—trying to limit
what he was taking until we could get him off pills and show
him that he could perform without them."

A few days later, after deliberating for fifty minutes, the
board found Dr. Nichopoulos guilty as charged.

Everything becomes as a dream:

The little stone lamb bade him to enumerate his sins, that
by the very utterance of admission they might be absolved. He
looked within himself and he began to speak, but he suddenly
remembered that demons delighted in assuming forms of
goodness, so he closed his mouth and his eyes to the lamb.
When he opened his eyes, he began to laugh. He calmly
searched his room for clues as to where he was. It did not take
him long to figure out that he was in Holland, a place well
known for its wooden shoes, tulips, and windmills.

When he arrived in Oklahoma City on the first day of June,
he was arrested. The men with the handcuffs told him that he
was being taken into custody under an old bench warrant that
had been issued after his failure to pay a $450,000 judgment

won against him in 1978 by a local nightclub owner named Cunningham.

Any fool could tell that there was no Cunningham and that the men with the handcuffs were not earthly lawmen.

When the reporter from the Associated Press questioned him—and what exactly, come to think of it, was this Associated Press, this elusive yet ubiquitous cabal whose inquisitors, year in and year out, seemed to arrive with prescience at the very moment of his every persecution?—Jerry Lee did not say that he knew himself to be in that ancient city that was the mother of harlots and abominations of the earth. "I like it here in Oklahoma," is all he said. "There's a lot of good-lookin' women here."

He telephoned Myra Gale at her home in Stone Mountain, Georgia. He told her that he loved her and that he wanted to marry her again. He sat in the dark and drank a beer. He thought of Jezebel, of how she was devoured by dogs and of how this pleased the Lord. He looked at the clock. He was forty-five years old.

It was Cleveland or Toledo. Wherever it was, it was dark and raining hard. He dialed room service, to get him a bottle, but there was no answer. He turned on the television set, but found nothing but static. The static took on a strange, dreamlike clarity, and he began to see a swarm of vile insects. These were the principal demons, loosed from the brass vessel of Solomon.

He read in the newspaper that yesterday the IRS had auctioned off all the wordly goods—cars and guns and jewels and gold—that they had seized from him. He read that the money

brought in by this auction did not equal his debt, and that the
IRS wanted more.

The snake, roused from its hibernation at the edge of the
lake, crept this Christmas morning to within a few yards of his
door. He could see by the white markings on the sides of its
black head that the snake was a moccasin, an old one. It was as
long as he was tall, and its thick triangular head was as large as
his fist.

If his arms had not been wrested from him, he would have
machine-gunned the big black bastard where it lay. But all he
had was a garden hoe.

The viper raised its ugly head and opened its mouth wide to
him, showing the great fangs that shot from its pallid gums.
He looked at that mouth, those fangs, and he swung the hoe.
He missed. The snake spat at him, then turned and crept
away, toward the lake and its deathlike season's sleep.

Every male child must be killed. Drench every cradle in
blood. When the mother takes the boy to her breast to suck,
let his male blood then redden the blade and splash down, like
so.

He stood before the window, facing west, and allowed himself to be blinded by the fleeting fierce brightness that preceded winter dusk in the Mississippi flatlands. He turned away
and wandered through his many hollow chambers. Twilight
came, then black night, but still they would not come: not
Elmo, nor Uncle Lee, nor the Old Man, nor the Judge, nor any
of them—not even Mamie's darling hawk-eyed boy.

They had all forsaken him, led him to this dark copse where
Satan and the Holy Ghost spilled the blood of their pitting—
led him here and forsaken him. He tried to tell the tales—

"Old Man Lewis," he began, feebly, haltingly, "was a hell of a man"—but there was no son to hear these words, nor strength to be summoned by their utterance; so his mouth fell still, and there was no sound but that of the Hecate wind that swept through De Soto County toward the rising river.

Index

INDEX

270

INDEX

Little Milton, 99
Lockwood, Roy, 133
Logan, Horace, 56, 58
London, Engl., 152–61, 178–79,
    180, 185–86, 222–23
London *Daily Sketch,* 156
London *Daily Herald,* 153,
    156–58, 162
London *Evening Star,* 158
"Lonesome Valley," 116
Long, Huey, 26–27
Los Angeles, Calif., 198–201, 239
Los Angeles Times, 200
Lott, Jimmy, 123
Love, Lloyd, 69
"Lovesick Blues," 56
Louis, Joe Hill, 99
"Louisiana Hayride, The,"55–56,88
Loyd, Robert, 2
Lymon, Frankie, 145

McCormack, Grover, 147
McGhee, Stick, 64
Mack, Ted, 67
McMahon, Ann, 220
McRae, Robert M., Jr., 257
Malito, Peter, 211, 220
Mangham, La., 10, 16, 78–79
Marshall, William, 199
"Matchbox," 114
May, Julius A., 85
"Mean Woman Blues," 137, 186
Melody Maker, 185
Memphis, Tenn., 98, 99–104,
    107, 108–10, 114–19, 123–24,
    163–64, 170, 171, 177–78ff.,
    210ff., 330, 333, 341–43, 346,

238, 245–47, 258–60. *See also*
    Sun Records; specific residents
Memphis *Press-Scimitar,* 115, 147,
    153–55, 163, 182
Memphis Slim and His House
    Rockers, 57
Mercury Records, 183, 195–96ff.,
    220ff., 237, 238, 242, 249
Meteor Records, 104
Milland, Ray, 199
Mills, Irving, 56
Milton, Roy, and His Solid
    Senders, 57
Minneapolis, Minn., 175
Miró, Don Estevan de, 8
Mitcham, Sallie, 82
Monkees, the, 202
Monroe, Bill, 116
Monroe, James, 9
Monroe, La., 8–10, 53, 67, 79–80
Morris, William, Agency, 151
Morrison, Jim, 202
"My Baby Don't Love No One but
    Me," 185
"My God Is Real," 73–74

Nashville, Tenn., 88–90, 183,
    184, 187, 195ff., 201–2,
    203–5, 220–21, 242, 248–49.
    See also specific residents
Nashville *Banner,* 247
Nashville Teens, 185
Nashville *Tennessean,* 212–13
Natchez, Miss., 81–82, 90ff.
Neal, Bob, 118, 119, 122
Nelson, C. A., 147
Nelson, Willie, 186

272

241–42, 243, 247–48, 259; and committing of JLL, 258; mother's death, 176–77

Swaggart, Minnie Bell Herron (mother), 22ff., 36, 141, death of, 176–77

Swaggart, Willie Harry, 22–23

Swaggart, Willie Leon, 22–23ff., 36, 140–41

Swan, Billy, 238

"Sweetheart, You Done Me Wrong," 116

"Take Me Out to the Ball Game," 189–90

Tamblyn, Russ, 143

Tarrant, Robert "Tarp," 190–93, 209–10, 231–32, 238–41

Taylor, Bill, 183

"Tell Me Why," 138

"That's All Right," 87

"There Is Power in the Blood," 78

Thing with Two Heads, The, 199

"33⅓ Revolutions Per Monkee," 202

Thompson, John, 104

Tobacco Road, 181

"Today" show, 146

"To Make Love Sweeter for You," 202

Tom and Jerry, 139

Tooting, Engl., 158, 159

Toronto *Daily Star,* 200

Treniers, the, 155

Trumpet Records, 87

Tubb, Ernest, 223

Turner, Ike, 99

United Press International, 133, 253

Van Eaton, James, 109, 118–19, 122, 129ff.

Van Story, Marcus, 123, 124

Variety, 137–38

Vicksburg, Miss., 9

Wagon Wheel (Natchez), 85–86, 90

Walker, La., 251

Walters, Lou, 166

Ward, Hedley, Trio, 155

Warner Brothers, 133

Waxahachie, Tex., 72–74

Weiss, Carl, 27

West, Mrs. (teacher), 47–48

"What'd I Say," 176, 183, 223

"What's Made Milwaukee Famous (Has Made a Loser Out of Me)," 201

WHBQ, 113

Wheeler, Onie, 122

Whitehead, Paul, 85, 86, 192

Whitman, Slim, 88, 133

Whitten, M. C., 140

"Whole Lotta Shakin' Goin' On," 93–94, 120–21ff., 125ff., 133, 137, 184, 186, 202, 224, 245

Wild Palms, The, 16

"Wild Side of Life, The," 86

Williams, Dave, 94–95

Williams, Hank, 55–56, 151, 176, 242, 243, 255

275

(